I0008337

101AI
The Ultimate Guide to Artificial Intelligence Mastery

Muneeb Ahmad

101AI: THE ULTIMATE GUIDE TO ARTIFICIAL
INTELLIGENCE MASTERY
Copyright © 2023 by Muneeb Ahmad
All rights reserved.

No part of this book may be reproduced, stored in a retrieval system, or transmitted in any form or by any means—electronic, mechanical, photocopying, recording, or otherwise—without prior written permission from the author or publisher, except for brief quotations in reviews or articles.

This book is a work of the author's original creation. Any resemblance to actual persons, living or dead, or actual events is purely coincidental.

Dedication

To my parents,
whose unwavering hard work and sacrifices ensured I had everything I needed to succeed in both education and profession.

To my brothers and sisters,
whose love and support began with my very first spoken words and continued steadfastly through school, college, and university.

To my wife,
whose constant support and encouragement have been my strength every step of the way.

To my children,
whose love and deep respect fill my heart with pride and joy every day.

This book is a tribute to you.

About the Author

Muneeb Ahmad is the founder of **101ai.net** and **PlayWithML.com**, two innovative AI/ML learning platforms designed to simplify artificial intelligence education through interactive visual tools, real-world applications, and real-world experiments. His mission is to make complex AI concepts accessible and engaging for students, educators, and AI enthusiasts.

In addition to his contributions to **AI education**, Muneeb serves as a **Senior API Architect**, where he has successfully led cross-functional teams and strategic initiatives to help organizations design, adopt, and scale their **API programs**. With a diverse background spanning roles such as Microservices Architect, **Enterprise Architect**, and Technical Product Manager, he brings deep expertise in modern technologies including Java, Spring Boot, AWS, and Kubernetes. His experience reflects a strong blend of architectural vision and hands-on technical leadership, enabling impactful digital transformation across enterprise environments.

Known for his creativity, leadership, and penchant for **kinesthetic learning**, Muneeb is not only a seasoned professional but also a mentor and evangelist who believes in giving back to the community. He has earned accolades through **research papers, patents, and achievement awards** that reflect his commitment to excellence.

Muneeb holds a BS degree in **Systems Engineering** and an MS degree in **Robotics Engineering**.

Table of Contents

Foreword

AI is one of the most profound technological transformations in history. Once confined to academic research and science fiction, it is now a driving force behind innovation, automation, and progress. From revolutionizing healthcare and finance to reshaping creativity and communication, AI is no longer the future—it is the present.

Despite its profound impact, AI remains an enigma to many. Questions about its mechanics, real-world applications, and ethical implications continue to fuel debate. For some, it represents boundless opportunities, for others, a formidable challenge. One thing is certain—understanding AI is no longer a choice but a necessity.

101AI - The Ultimate Guide to Artificial Intelligence Mastery bridges the gap between complexity and accessibility. This book is more than a technical guide—it is a companion for anyone seeking to understand AI's fundamentals, potential, and impact. Whether you are a student, entrepreneur, developer, or a curious learner, this book provides the knowledge and tools to navigate the AI revolution with confidence.

Preface

Artificial Intelligence (AI) is no longer a distant concept—it is here, transforming how we live, work, and think. From recommendation systems to healthcare innovations, AI has become an integral part of modern technology. Yet, for many, it remains a complex field filled with mathematical formulas, abstract concepts, and evolving frameworks.

This book was born from a passion to simplify AI learning and make it accessible to all—students, developers, and curious minds alike. Through **101ai.net** and **PlayWithML.com**, I've seen firsthand the power of interactive, visual learning. This book follows the same philosophy, breaking down complex ideas with clear explanations, real-world examples, and hands-on code implementations.

We begin with data preparation and core machine learning algorithms, progressing to gradient descent, neural networks, and deep learning. Later chapters explore specialized areas like computer vision, audio processing, and natural language processing (NLP). This structured approach ensures a seamless learning journey from beginner to advanced AI concepts.

But this book is more than just theory—it's about application. You'll work with real-world datasets, build models, and develop an intuitive understanding of AI systems. The goal is not just to teach AI, but to empower you to experiment, innovate, and solve real-world problems.

AI is reshaping the future. Whether you're here to learn, research, or build, this book will be your companion in mastering AI.

Introduction

AI is no longer a futuristic dream—it is shaping the world today. From self-driving cars and virtual assistants to breakthroughs in healthcare and finance, AI is transforming industries. But how does it work? What are its capabilities, and how can we harness its potential?

101AI - The Ultimate Guide to Artificial Intelligence Mastery serves as your roadmap into AI, whether you're a beginner or a professional looking to refine your skills. This book simplifies complex AI concepts, offering practical insights, real-world applications, and hands-on projects.

What you'll explore:

- AI fundamentals: machine learning, deep learning, and neural networks.

- Real-world applications across industries.

- Practical techniques to build AI-powered solutions.

Chapter 1: Introduction to AI and Data Preparation

Artificial Intelligence (AI) is transforming industries, from healthcare and finance to transportation and retail. AI-powered algorithms detect diseases early, personalize treatment plans, and predict epidemic outbreaks. In finance, AI analyzes transactions in real time, identifying fraud faster than human analysts. Manufacturing benefits from predictive maintenance, preventing costly equipment failures, while retail leverages AI for personalized customer experiences and optimized supply chains.

Unlike sci-fi portrayals of humanoid robots, AI is a practical tool solving real-world problems, seamlessly integrating into our daily lives.

The Evolution and Branches of AI

AI has evolved from simple rule-based algorithms to complex, intelligent systems. This section explores its journey and key branches, including machine learning (ML) and deep learning (DL).

Machine Learning (ML) enables computers to learn from data without explicit programming, automating tasks once thought to require human intelligence.

Deep Learning (DL), a subset of ML, mimics the human brain's neural networks, excelling in tasks like image recognition and natural language processing with remarkable accuracy.

AI's rapid advancement continues to reshape industries, making it an essential field to understand and master.

Beyond Automation: AI's Role in Complex Problem-Solving

One of AI's most compelling attributes is its ability to solve complex problems that traditional methods cannot handle. For instance, climate scientists use AI to analyze vast amounts of climate data, enabling more accurate predictions and helping devise strategies to combat climate change. Urban planners employ AI to optimize traffic flow in congested cities, reducing emissions and improving public safety. By processing and analyzing immense data sets, AI uncovers insights that humans may overlook, offering solutions to some of the world's most pressing challenges.

Setting the Stage for Exploration

In this chapter, we'll explore how AI works behind the scenes, making these incredible feats possible. We'll look at the development and workings of AI systems and discuss their societal impact. As you progress through this book, you'll see that AI is not a monolithic concept, but a diverse field filled with powerful techniques and methods. By understanding the basics of data preparation and the fundamentals of AI models, you'll be better equipped to grasp the significance of AI in driving our world forward.

Practical Example: Predicting House Prices

To begin our AI journey with a hands-on approach, consider this practical example: *predicting house prices*. We have a dataset containing the size of the house in square feet, the number of bedrooms, and the corresponding price. By training a neural network model on this data, we aim to predict the price of a house based on its size and number of bedrooms. This example will take us through the entire process, from data preprocessing to model training and prediction, as illustrated in Figure 1.1.

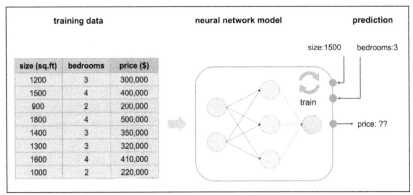

Figure 1.1: Overview of the House Price Prediction Model

Another Example: Predicting Car Prices

Another practical application involves predicting car prices. Here, the dataset includes the engine size, horsepower, and price of various cars. Training a neural network model to predict the car price based on these features further illustrates the importance of data scaling and model training, as shown in Figure 1.2.

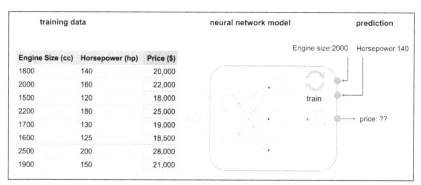

Figure 1.2: Car Price Prediction Model Overview

Importance of Data Scaling in AI

Data scaling is important for accurate and high-performing AI models. In this section, we'll explain why data scaling is necessary in machine learning algorithms. Scaling guarantees that all features contribute equally to the model's learning process, avoiding any biases towards certain features due to differences in scale. We'll look at how data that is not scaled properly can lead to inaccurate results and lengthier training periods. This underscores the significance of preparing data appropriately before putting it to use.

To further illustrate the importance of data scaling, consider the student test score prediction example. We have a dataset containing the number of hours studied, the number of practice tests taken, and the corresponding test scores. By scaling these features, the model can make more accurate predictions about future test scores, as depicted in Figure 1.3.

Without scaling, the model might incorrectly assume that one feature (e.g., hours studied) is more important than another (e.g., practice tests) simply because of its larger numeric range. Scaling eliminates this bias by putting all features on a level playing field. This becomes especially important in neural networks, where unscaled data can lead to slow convergence and suboptimal learning outcomes.

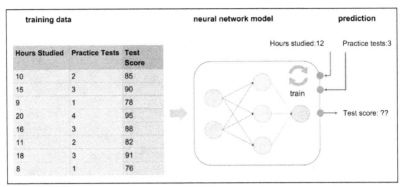

Figure 1.3: Student Test Score Prediction Model

Methods of Data Scaling: Normalization and Standardization

There are two main ways to adjust data: normalization and standardization. Normalization, also called min-max scaling, changes feature values to occupy a range of [0, 1] or [-1, 1], decreasing the influence of unusual values on the model. In contrast, standardization modifies data to contain a mean of zero and a standard deviation of one, aligning it with a standard normal distribution. We will examine when each method is best and how it affects AI model performance, giving you a useful guide for applying them to data preparation.

Let's say we need to convert the below data, which is a list of test scores of a group of students, to its normalize and standard form

Student scores:

85, 86, 100, 76, 81, 93, 84, 99, 71, 69, 93, 85, 81, 87, 89

Below is the formula to compute the normalized form of the dataset:

$$normalized\ dataset = \frac{data - min}{max - min}$$

In the above equation the symbol *'data'* represents each data element in the dataset, *'min'* is the minimum value and *'max'* is the maximum value of the dataset. From the above dataset, we can get the *min* and *max* values as below:

min = 69
max = 100

Using these values of *min*, *max* and *data* we can calculate the *normalized dataset*, rounded to 2 decimal places, as below

normalized dataset:

> 0.52, 0.55, 1.00, 0.23, 0.39, 0.77, 0.48, 0.97, 0.06, 0.00, 0.77, 0.52, 0.39, 0.58, 0.65

Next, let's convert the data set to the standardized dataset format. Below is the formula:

$$standardized\ dataset = \frac{data - mean}{std}$$

In the above equation the symbol *'data'* represents each data element in the dataset, *'mean'* is the average, and *'std'* is the standard deviation of the dataset. Below are the formulas to calculate the mean and standard deviation:

$$mean = \frac{1}{n} \sum_{i=1}^{n} data_i$$

$$std = \sqrt{\frac{1}{n} \sum_{i=1}^{n} (data_i - mean)^2}$$

Using the above dataset and applying these formulas, we compute the *mean* and standard deviation (*std*) as below:

> **mean** = 85.27
> **std** = 8.70

By substituting these values of *mean* and *std* in the 'standardized dataset' formula we get the below converted dataset.

standardized dataset:

> -0.03, 0.08, 1.69, -1.07, -0.49, 0.89, -0.15, 1.58, -1.64, -1.87, 0.89, -0.03, -0.49, 0.20, 0.43

Practical Application: House Price Prediction Example

Returning to our house price prediction example, we preprocess the training data by scaling the size and number of bedrooms. This step is crucial for effective model training.

Data Preprocessing Steps:

- Scaling Data: Ensure that all features are on a comparable scale.
- Converting to Tensors: Prepare the scaled data for the neural network model

As shown in **Figure 1.4**, the data preprocessing and model training workflow include scaling the data, converting it to tensors, defining the model architecture, and training the model over multiple epochs.

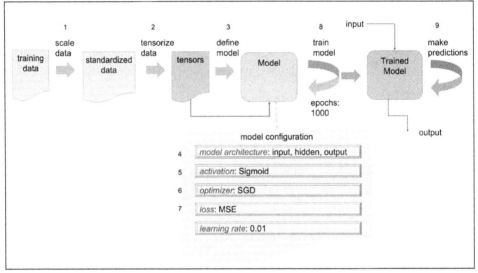

Figure 1.4: Neural Network Model Training Workflow

The workflow illustrated in Figure 1.4 outlines the end-to-end process of preparing data for a neural network model. It begins with raw training data, which is first scaled to ensure consistency across features and then standardized to fit a common distribution. This standardized data is then converted into tensors, a format required for input into neural networks. Once the data is in tensor form, the model is defined with specific architecture and hyperparameters. The training phase involves feeding the data through the network repeatedly over multiple epochs, allowing the model to iteratively adjust its weights and biases to minimize prediction errors. The result is a trained model capable of making predictions on new, unseen data with improved accuracy.

Model Architecture and Training:

The neural network model used for predicting house prices consists of three main layers. While the structure is outlined below, the underlying architecture and inner workings of the model—such as how weights are updated, how layers interact, and the role of backpropagation—will be explored in greater detail in a later chapter dedicated to neural networks.

- Input Layer: Takes the standardized features.
- Hidden Layer: Uses the Sigmoid activation function.
- Output Layer: Outputs the predicted house price.

The model is configured with:

- Activation Function: **Sigmoid**
- Optimizer: **Stochastic Gradient Descent (SGD)**
- Loss Function: **Mean Squared Error (MSE)**
- Learning Rate: **0.01**

Each of these configuration components plays a critical role in how the model learns and performs. While they are introduced here briefly, concepts like activation functions, optimizers, loss functions, and learning rates will be discussed in greater depth in subsequent chapters to build a solid understanding of their significance and application in AI modeling.

Training the Model:

We train the model over multiple epochs, where weights and biases are adjusted to minimize the loss function. This iterative process helps the model learn from the data, as depicted in Figure 1.5, which illustrates the flow of information through the neural network layers during training.

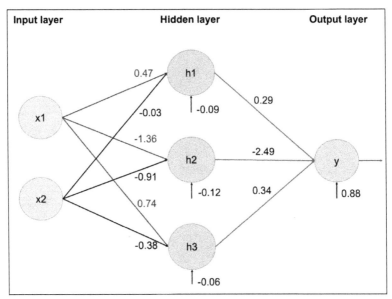

Figure 1.5: Neural Network Architecture with Weights

Prediction Flow in a Trained Model:

After training, the standardized input features are fed into the neural network to produce a standardized output. This output is then converted back to the original scale to get the final prediction, such as the price of a house. The entire prediction flow, including how input features are standardized and later converted back to their original scale, is illustrated in Figure 1.6.

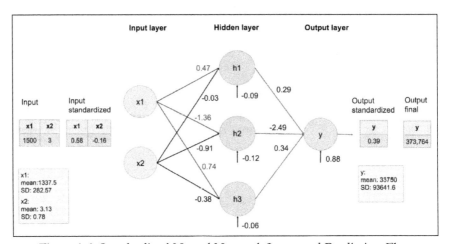

Figure 1.6: Standardized Neural Network Input and Prediction Flow

Summary

We delved into the evolution of AI, highlighting the distinctions between machine learning (ML) and deep learning (DL), and discussed how these branches solve complex real-world problems. We also examined AI's significant impact on society, from diagnosing diseases and automating financial processes to optimizing urban infrastructure and addressing climate challenges.

To ground our theoretical understanding, we introduced practical examples, such as predicting house and car prices, to demonstrate the importance of data preparation in building accurate AI models. We emphasized the necessity of data scaling, explaining how normalization and standardization transform raw data into a suitable form for model training. Through detailed formulas and datasets, we illustrated how these methods ensure features contribute equally, enhancing model performance and reducing biases.

The chapter concluded with an overview of a simple neural network model for predicting house prices, detailing its architecture, training process, and prediction flow. By the end, readers should have a foundational understanding of data preparation and AI's capabilities, setting the stage for deeper exploration in subsequent chapters.

Chapter 2: Basics of Machine Learning Algorithms

Machine learning, a subset of artificial intelligence, involves algorithms and statistical models that computers use to perform specific tasks without explicit instructions. It relies on patterns and inference rather than fixed rules. At its core, machine learning uses mathematical models to make predictions or decisions based on data. Understanding the basics of how these algorithms work is crucial, especially as they increasingly influence our daily lives and numerous industries. This chapter focuses on fundamental concepts, with a particular emphasis on understanding how machine learning models learn from data

We'll start with one of the simplest and most widely used algorithms: Linear Regression. Through practical examples and step-by-step explanations, we'll lay the groundwork for understanding more complex models.

Introduction to Linear Regression and its applications

Linear regression is a popular and basic machine learning method. It's often used as a foundation for predictive modeling in various fields. This section explains what linear regression is, where it stands in the broader machine learning context, and how it predicts a dependent variable's behavior based on one or more independent variables. In this section, we will also be discussing real-world examples of linear regression, including predicting housing prices and estimating stock market trends. Linear regression is an important tool in machine learning because it is simple, easy to understand, and has a foundation in statistical theory.

To demonstrate the linear regression let's consider the below example of data for the variables x and y.

x	50, 60, 70, 80, 90, 100, 110, 120, 130, 140, 150
y	7, 8, 8, 9, 9, 9, 10, 11, 14, 14, 15

Let's assume that this data can be represented in the form of a line equation as below:

$$y' = ax+b$$

Here the **y'** (or y-prime) represents the predicted values which we can compare with the actual values **y**.

Let's say we initialize the line equation with some arbitrary parameter values of a and b as below

$$a = 0.02$$
$$b = 8.78$$

With these values the line equation becomes:

$$y' = 0.02x + 8.78$$

Now let's plot the x-y values a s scatter 2D graph and the line graph of the above line equation as shown in Figure 2.1:

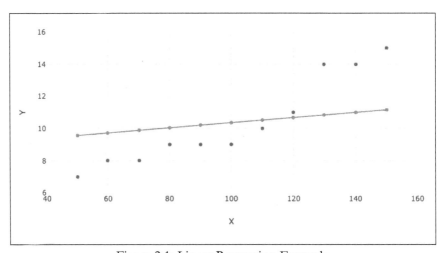

Figure 2.1: Linear Regression Example

In this chart the input x, y data is shown as a scatter plot with dots and the solid line shows the regression line approximating and representing the data.

Our goal is to use some algorithm to find the values of a and b that best fit the data. This is where the linear regression technique comes in. The process of finding the most appropriate values of a and b is known as "fitting the model to the data". In linear regression, this fitting is usually done using a method called "least squares". This method minimizes the sum of the squares of the differences (called residuals) between the predicted and actual values in the data set.

Least Squares Method

The least squares method calculates the optimal values of a (slope) and b (y-intercept) such that the sum of the squared differences between the predicted and actual values is minimized. Mathematically, it aims to solve the following:

$$\min_{a,b} \sum_{i=1}^{n} (y_i - (ax_i + b))^2$$

Where:

y_i and x_i are the actual observed values from the dataset,

n is the number of observations in the dataset,

$ax_i + b$ is the prediction made by our linear model.

When we apply the Least Squares method to our data, we calculate values for a and b that best fit our data points. After this calculation, our line equation looks like as below:

$y' = 0.08x + 2.47$

The below graph (Figure 2.2) shows how the above line equation, shown as a solid line, seems to fit the input data shown as dots.

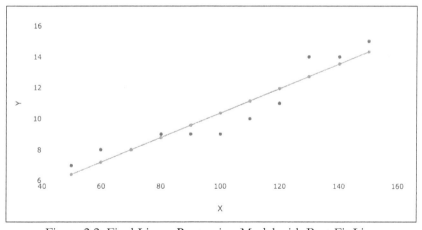

Figure 2.2: Final Linear Regression Model with Best Fit Line

Understanding Loss, Metrics, and their significance in model evaluation

In machine learning, evaluating and improving model performance depends on understanding loss and metrics. This section explains the significance of loss functions for regression (such as Mean Squared Error) and for classification (such as Cross-Entropy Loss). Metrics like accuracy, precision, and recall also play a critical role, and we'll explore why they're necessary. We'll talk about how loss functions guide the training process by measuring the model's errors, and how metrics help to interpret the model's performance in a practical way. These concepts are essential for creating efficient machine learning models since they give feedback that's needed to adjust models and make informed decisions about their implementation.

Consider the dataset presented in the table below, consisting of columns x, y, and y':

x	y	y'
1	1	3
2	4	5
3	8	7
4	10	9
5	10	11
6	15	13

Figure 2.3: Sample Dataset

Upon performing a linear regression analysis, we hypothesize the relationship between x and y' to be:

$$y' = 1 + 2x$$

In the above table and the equation, y' represents the predicted values, while y denotes the true output values.

In evaluating the performance of our regression model, we'll delve into four key metrics: Mean Square Error (MSE), Mean Absolute Error (MAE), Cosine Proximity, and Cosine Distance. Notably, MSE and MAE fall under the category of loss functions, while Cosine Proximity and Cosine Distance are considered evaluation metrics.

Alterations to the y-values in the table will correspondingly impact the computed values for our loss functions and metrics.

The formulas to compute these four metrics are as follows:

$$MSE = \frac{1}{n} \sum_{i=1}^{n} (y_i - y_i')^2$$

$$MAE = \frac{1}{n} \sum_{i=1}^{n} |y_i - y_i'|$$

$$CosineProximity = \frac{\sum_{i=1}^{n} y_i \cdot y_i'}{\sqrt{\sum_{i=1}^{n} y_i^2} \cdot \sqrt{\sum_{i=1}^{n} y_i'^2}}$$

$$CosineDistance = 1 - CosineProximity$$

Mean Square Error (MSE): This calculates the average squared difference between the predicted and actual values.

Mean Absolute Error (MAE): This computes the average absolute difference between the predicted and actual values.

Cosine Proximity: This metric gauge the similarity between two vectors by determining the cosine of the angle between them. Within machine learning, it offers insights into the closeness of two samples or feature vectors.

Cosine Distance: Essentially the inverse of Cosine Proximity, it quantifies the dissimilarity between two vectors.

Using the above formulas, we calculate the values of these quantities as below:

y	y'	error (y - y')	(error)²	abs(error)	y.y'	y²	y'²	|y|.|y'|
1	3	-2	4	2	3	1	9	3
4	5	-1	1	1	20	16	25	20
8	7	1	1	1	56	64	49	56
10	9	1	1	1	90	100	81	90
10	11	-1	1	1	110	100	121	110
15	13	2	4	2	195	225	169	195
			mean= 2.00	mean= 1.33	sum 474	sqr(sum) 22.49	sqr(sum) 21.31	sum= 474
			MSE	2.00			Cosine Proximity	0.99
			MAE	1.33			Cosine Distance	0.01

Figure 2.4: Sample Dataset

For better comprehension of the loss function, observe a scatter plot that compares our dataset with the regression line. This will give you a clear view of how close (or far apart) the actual data points are from the regression line.

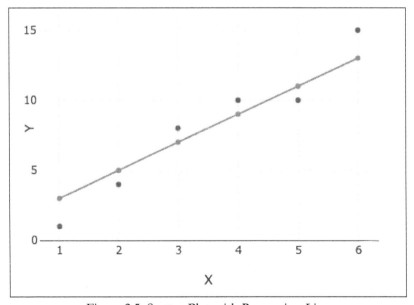

Figure 2.5: Scatter Plot with Regression Line

Summary

In this chapter, we delved into the basics of linear regression, a foundational machine learning method vital for predictive modeling across various disciplines. At its core, linear regression predicts the behavior of a dependent variable based on one or multiple independent variables. It finds extensive applications in real-world scenarios, such as forecasting housing prices or estimating stock market trends.

Using an example dataset, we explored how data can be represented through the equation $y' = ax+b$. In this context y' represents the predicted outcomes, which can be contrasted with the actual values y. A central goal in linear regression is determining the optimal values of a and b that best fit the data—a process known as model fitting. The least squares method is commonly used to achieve this. It minimizes the sum of squared residuals, or differences, between the predicted and actual data points. By applying this method, we found the best-fit line equation for our example dataset, effectively modeling the relationship between variables.

We also emphasized the significance of loss functions and metrics in evaluating and refining machine learning models. Various loss functions, like Mean Squared Error (MSE) and Mean Absolute Error (MAE), are used to measure the model's performance. Additionally, evaluation metrics such as Cosine Proximity and Cosine Distance are crucial for assessing how well the model captures the data's underlying patterns. These tools are paramount in gauging a model's accuracy and efficiency, providing essential feedback for adjusting and enhancing implementation.

Through linear regression, one can capture relationships within data and make informed predictions. As we've seen, it's not just about drawing the best-fit line but also understanding and quantifying how well it represents the data, thus laying the groundwork for more complex predictive modeling techniques.

Chapter 3: Diving Deep into Gradient Descent

Gradient descent is a cornerstone in the world of machine learning and artificial intelligence, forming the backbone of many optimization and learning algorithms. This chapter delves into the intricacies and nuances of gradient descent, uncovering its fundamental principles and examining its practical applications.

The concept of Gradient Descent

Figure 3.1: Illustration of Gradient Descent Concept

Gradient Descent can be compared to a treasure hunter's journey to find the lowest point in a valley. Imagine being blindfolded and placed on top of a mountain. Your mission? To find the lowest point possible. Your only guide is the slope you feel under your feet or in your hands, forcing you to take tiny, incremental steps downhill in the sharpest direction you can perceive. As you repeat this process-each step a small adjustment in direction-you gradually descend closer to the bottom of the valley. In machine learning, the gradient descent algorithm works in a similar way. Here, the valley symbolizes the error or loss in our model's predictions, and our goal is to minimize that error. The slope at each point is indicative of the gradient, which guides us to the path of steepest descent.

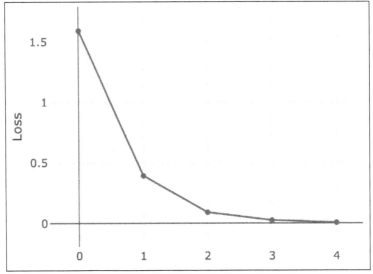

Figure 3.2: Gradient Descent Process

This above graph illustrates the "treasure hunt" machine learning process, where each learning step or epoch aims to minimize the value of the loss function. It visually represents the journey of gradient descent, with the x-axis representing the number of epochs and the y-axis representing the value of the loss function. As the epochs progress, one can observe an exponential decrease in the loss function, demonstrating the effectiveness of the algorithm in optimizing and reducing errors over time.

Consider a straightforward two-dimensional x-y dataset:

x	0.2, 0.4, 0.6, 0.8, 1.0, 1.2
y	0.18, 0.32, 0.42, 0.48, 0.58, 0.72

We aim to fit this data with a linear equation:

$$\hat{y} = ax + b$$

Let's choose the initial values of the parameters a, b and the learning rate (alpha) as below:

$a = 1$
$b = 1$
$alpha = 0.1$

This learning rate (alpha) in gradient descent is like the size of the steps we take as we descend the mountain; too large a step might overshoot the valley, and too small a step might take too long or get stuck in a small dip.

We calculate some variables values as shown in the below table:

x	y	$\hat{y}$	$\hat{y} - y$	$2(\hat{y} - y)$	$(\hat{y} - y)^2$
0.2	0.18	1.2	1.02	2.04	1.040
0.4	0.32	1.4	1.08	2.16	1.166
0.6	0.42	1.6	1.18	2.36	1.392
0.8	0.48	1.8	1.32	2.64	1.742
1.0	0.58	2.0	1.42	2.84	2.016
1.2	0.72	2.2	1.48	2.96	2.190
				Average	**1.591**

Figure 3.3: Initial Data Points and Predicted Values

This table contains x and y values, along with their predicted counterparts ($\hat{y}$), the difference ($\hat{y} - y$), twice the difference ($2(\hat{y} - y)$), and the squared difference (($\hat{y} - y)^2$), which is used to compute the loss.

The loss, representing the average squared error, is calculated as:

$$L = \frac{1}{n} \sum (\hat{y} - y)^2$$

The computed loss (L) is: **1.591**

Updating values of a and b:

$$a = a - \alpha \frac{\partial L}{\partial a}$$

$$b = b - \alpha \frac{\partial L}{\partial b}$$

We now compute the partial derivatives or gradients. To compute the gradients, we apply the **chain rule** from calculus. In the context of training neural networks, we often need to compute how the loss function L changes with respect to model parameters like a. However, since the loss L is not directly a function of a but rather depends on the predicted output $\hat{y}$ which in turn depends on a, we use the **chain rule** to break down as below:

$$\frac{\partial L}{\partial a} = \frac{\partial L}{\partial \hat{y}} \frac{\partial \hat{y}}{\partial a}$$

$$\frac{\partial L}{\partial \hat{y}} = \frac{1}{n} \sum 2(\hat{y} - y)$$

$$\frac{\partial \hat{y}}{\partial a} = \frac{1}{n} \sum x$$

While deriving the above equations, we used the below intermediate steps:

$$\hat{y} = ax + b$$

$$\frac{\partial \hat{y}}{\partial a} = x$$

In practice, we usually compute the **average gradient** over all n training examples in the dataset.

$$\frac{\partial \hat{y}}{\partial a} = \frac{1}{n} \sum_{i=1}^{n} x_i$$

$$\frac{\partial \hat{y}}{\partial a} = \frac{1}{n} \sum x$$

$$L = \frac{1}{n} \sum (\hat{y} - y)^2$$

$$\frac{\partial}{\partial \hat{y}} (\hat{y} - y)^2 = 2(\hat{y} - y)$$

Now, similarly we compute the gradient of L with respect to parameter b.

$$\frac{\partial L}{\partial b} = \frac{\partial L}{\partial \hat{y}} \frac{\partial \hat{y}}{\partial b}$$

$$\frac{\partial L}{\partial \hat{y}} = \frac{1}{n} \sum 2(\hat{y} - y)$$

$$\frac{\partial \hat{y}}{\partial b} = 1$$

Using the values from the table and plugin them into the above equations we come up with the below values:

$\partial L / \partial \hat{y} = 2.5$ $\partial \hat{y} / \partial a = 0.7$ $\partial \hat{y} / \partial b = 1$

$\partial L / \partial a = 1.75$ $\partial L / \partial b = 2.5$

$a = 0.825$ $b = 0.75$

Below is the X-Y plot of the input data and the graph of the regression line at this initial stage:

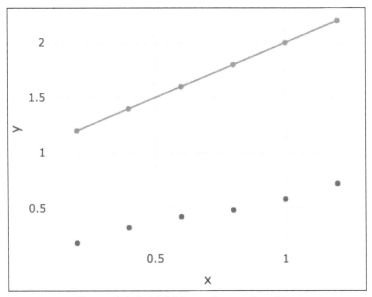

Figure 3.4: Initial Linear Regression Line

This chart displays a scatter plot with observed data (as dots) and an initial linear regression line (as solid line). The line's poor fit at this stage suggests the need for further training or adjustment for a more accurate model.

Given that the value of a and b are 0.825 and 0.75 at the initial stage, the equation of the regression line is as below:

$$\hat{y} = 0.825x + 0.75$$

Now, if we want to iterate through the gradient descent function, we must continue to compute the values of the partial derivatives and the new values of a and b at each iteration or epoch. As the line converges to represent the input data fitted to a straight line, the value of the loss function will begin to converge. Once the value of the loss function becomes very low, close to zero, then the final values of a and b are the values that represent the perfectly fitted regression line.

The below table captures the progressive updates of various parameter values and the corresponding loss during each iteration of the gradient descent process.

Learning rate (α) = 0.1

Iteration	a	b	$\partial L/\partial a$	$\partial L/\partial b$	updated a	updated b	Loss (L)
1	1	1	1.750	2.500	0.93	0.955	5.20
2	0.93	0.955	1.229	1.755	0.702	0.575	0.782
3	0.702	0.575	0.862	1.232	0.616	0.451	0.384
...	...	...	...	...	...	...	...
13	...	...	0.018	0.025	0.417	0.167	0.001
...	...	...	...	...	...	...	...

Figure 3.5: Parameter Update Table

It's clear from the table that as the iterations progress, the values of $\partial L/\partial a$ and $\partial L/\partial b$ are decreasing, leading to an update in 'a' and 'b' values, which in turn results in a significant reduction in the loss (L). This trend is indicative of the gradient descent algorithm successfully moving towards a minimum of the loss function. The change from iteration 2 to 3, for instance, shows a notable decrease in loss, suggesting that the learning rate and direction of the gradient descent are effectively optimizing the parameters. Iteration 13 demonstrates a very low loss, indicating that the algorithm is close to finding the optimal values of a and b for the given problem.

The below chart demonstrates how the Loss (L) is reduced at each iteration.

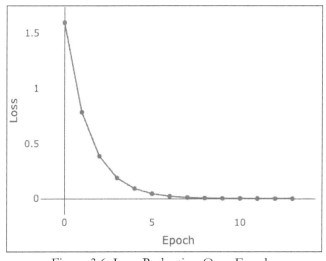

Figure 3.6: Loss Reduction Over Epochs

After 13 iterations the equation of the regression line becomes as below:

$$\hat{y} = 0.417x + 0.167$$

The below chart shows the input x-y data points and the regression line fitted to the data.

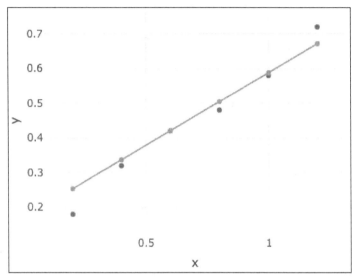

Figure 3.7: Final Regression Line Fit

Please note that the data points are close to the regression line, suggesting a good fit.

The essence of the gradient descent algorithm in machine learning is to iteratively adjust the parameters of a model to minimize the loss function-the difference between the predicted output and the actual output. Through successive iterations, as seen by the changes from the initial equation to the updated one and the movement of the regression line in the graphs, the model gradually becomes more accurate and reliable. This method, which is fundamental to machine learning, illustrates how continuous improvement and fine-tuning are critical to developing effective predictive models. Just as a treasure hunter gets closer to the treasure with each step, gradient descent moves incrementally toward the optimal solution, symbolizing the continuous journey of learning and improvement in AI and data science.

Stochastic Gradient Descent and its advantages

As covered in the previous section, the Gradient Descent is a fundamental optimization algorithm used in machine learning to minimize the loss function, which represents the error between the predicted outcomes by our model and the actual values. The process involves computing the gradient, which is essentially the slope of the loss function at a given point, by considering every single example within the dataset. By understanding the direction and steepness of this slope, we can adjust the model's parameters—such as weights in a neural network—so that with each iteration, they inch closer to the optimal values that minimize the error. This method is particularly efficient when dealing with smaller datasets.

However, as datasets grow increasingly large, which is common in the era of big data, the traditional Gradient Descent can become computationally expensive and time-consuming. It requires processing all examples in the dataset to make a single update to the model's parameters, which can be inefficient when dealing with vast numbers of samples. In scenarios where datasets contain thousands or even millions of examples, Stochastic Gradient Descent (SGD) becomes a more viable alternative. SGD tackles the problem by updating the model's parameters based on the gradient of the loss function calculated from a randomly selected subset of data, rather than the entire dataset. This stochastic approach introduces noise into the parameter updates, which can help the model to escape local minima and potentially find a better overall solution more quickly than the traditional method. It's a compromise that leverages computational efficiency and speed at the cost of a higher variance in the updates, which often requires careful tuning of the learning rate and other hyperparameters to achieve the best results.

x	y	ŷ	ŷ - y	2 (ŷ - y)	2 (ŷ - y)²
0.2	0.18	1.2	1.02	2.04	1.040
0.4	0.32	1.4	1.08	2.16	1.166
0.6	0.42	1.6	1.18	2.36	1.392
0.8	0.48	1.8	1.32	2.64	1.742
1.0	0.58	2.0	1.42	2.84	2.016
1.2	0.72	2.2	1.48	2.96	2.190

a	0.825
b	0.750

Figure 3.8: Stochastic Gradient Descent Overview

In the Stochastic Gradient Descent algorithm, instead of considering the entire dataset at once, we pick a small subset of examples from the dataset and calculate the gradient and other parameters like a and b based on that subset of examples only. We repeat this process over the entire dataset. Typically, the subset examples are selected randomly. Due to this random dataset aspect of the algorithm, it is called "stochastic," which means involving a random component. The subset of examples is called a batch.

Let's consider the same example we covered in the Gradient Descent section of this chapter with the following values of x, y, ŷ, a, b and alpha.

x: 0.2, 0.4, 0.6, 0.8, 1.0, 1.2

y: 0.18, 0.32, 0.42, 0.48, 0.58, 0.72

$ŷ$ = ax + b

a = 1

b = 1

$alpha$ = 0.1

As in the Stochastic Gradient Descent algorithm there is a concept of batch which is the number of data samples used in calculating the Gradient Descent parameters, we choose the batch size for this example as below:

batch size = 2

Let's create a table of x, y, ŷ, and other parameters and variables just like we did for the Gradient Descent algorithm. We start with porting the x and y data to the table. Next, as the batch size is 2, we calculate the $\hat{y}$ values for the first 2 data samples only by using the initial values of a = 1, and b = 1 and the equation $\hat{y}$ = ax + b.

Epoch: 0   Batch: 0   a = 1   b = 1   Batch size: 2   alpha = 0.1

x	y	$\hat{y}$	$\hat{y}$ - y	Loss (L)	$\partial L/\partial a$	$\partial L/\partial b$	updated a	updated b
0.2	0.18	1.2						
0.4	0.32	1.4						
0.6	0.42							
0.8	0.48							
1.0	0.58							
1.2	0.72							

Figure 3.9: First Batch Calculation in SGD

Next, we calculate the values of $\hat{y}$ - y, Loss (L), $\partial L/\partial a$, $\partial L/\partial a$, updated a, and updated b by using the Gradient Descent formulas discussed in the previous section. Please note that these formulas require the summation (Σ) of values and the number of data samples (n) in the calculation. In Scholastic Gradient Descent the summation and the sample count scope is limited to one batch only and not to the whole dataset.

This means for the first batch (of first epoch), Batch 0, we calculate the values of columns $\hat{y}$ - y, Loss (L), and others by computing the column sums for the first two rows of the data table and averaging it for two data samples (or dividing the sums by 2). The below table shows all the column values for this first epoch and first batch. For example, below is how we calculated some of these values:

$\hat{y}$ - y = ((1.2 - 0.18) + (1.4 - 0.32)) / 2 = **1.05**

Loss = ((1.2 - 0.18)² + (1.4 - 0.32)²) / 2 = **1.103**

Epoch: 0   Batch: 0   a = 1   b = 1   Batch size: 2   alpha = 0.1

x	y	$\hat{y}$	$\hat{y}$ - y	Loss (L)	$\partial L/\partial a$	$\partial L/\partial b$	updated a	updated b

0.2	0.18	1.2						
0.4	0.32	1.4	**1.05**	**1.103**	**0.63**	**2.10**	**0.937**	**0.790**
0.6	0.42							
0.8	0.48							
1.0	0.58							
1.2	0.72							

Figure 3.10: SGD Batch Update Process

We use the below formula to calculate the values of Loss (L), $\partial L/\partial a$, $\partial L/\partial a$, updated a, and updated b. Please note that only data from the first two rows is used to calculate these values and n = 2.

$$L = \tfrac{1}{n} \sum (\hat{y} - y)^2$$

$$\frac{\partial L}{\partial a} = \frac{\partial L}{\partial \hat{y}} \frac{\partial \hat{y}}{\partial a}$$

$$\frac{\partial L}{\partial \hat{y}} = \tfrac{1}{n} \sum 2(\hat{y} - y)$$

$$\frac{\partial \hat{y}}{\partial a} = \tfrac{1}{n} \sum x$$

$$\frac{\partial L}{\partial b} = \frac{\partial L}{\partial \hat{y}} \frac{\partial \hat{y}}{\partial b}$$

$$\frac{\partial L}{\partial \hat{y}} = \tfrac{1}{n} \sum 2(\hat{y} - y)$$

$$\frac{\partial \hat{y}}{\partial b} = 1$$

$$a = a - \alpha \frac{\partial L}{\partial a}$$

$$b = b - \alpha \frac{\partial L}{\partial b}$$

The below tables shows values of all the parameters at various stages of epochs and batches. Please note how the Loss (L) is decreased as we go through epochs and batches.

Epoch: 0   Batch: 1   a = 0.937   b = 0.790   Batch size: 2   alpha = 0.1

x	y	ŷ	ŷ - y	Loss (L)	∂L/∂a	∂L/∂b	updated a	updated b
0.2	0.18	1.2						
0.4	0.32	1.4	1.05	1.103	0.63	2.10	0.937	0.790
0.6	0.42	1.352						
0.8	0.48	1.540	**0.996**	**0.996**	**1.394**	**1.992**	**0.798**	**0.591**
1.0	0.58							
1.2	0.72							

Figure 3.11: Loss Reduction in SGD

Epoch: 0   Batch: 2   a = 0.798   b = 0.591   Batch size: 2   alpha = 0.1

x	y	ŷ	ŷ - y	Loss (L)	∂L/∂a	∂L/∂b	updated a	updated b
0.2	0.18	1.2						
0.4	0.32	1.4	1.05	1.103	0.63	2.10	0.937	0.790
0.6	0.42	1.352						
0.8	0.48	1.540	0.996	0.996	1.394	1.992	0.798	0.591
1.0	0.58	1.388						
1.2	0.72	1548	**0.818**	**0.669**	**1.800**	**1.636**	**0.618**	**0.427**

Figure 3.12: SGD Progression Across Epochs

Epoch: 3   Batch: 1   a = 0.456   b = 0.166   Batch size: 2   alpha = 0.1

x	y	y	ŷ - y	Loss (L)	∂L/∂a	∂L/∂b	updated a	updated b
0.2	0.18	1.2						
0.4	0.32	1.4	…	…	…	…	…	…

0.6	0.42	0.439						
0.8	0.48	0.531	**0.035**	**0.001**	**0.049**	**0.070**	**0.451**	**0.159**
1.0	0.58	1.388						
1.2	0.72	1548	...	...	...	...	...	...

Figure 3.13: Final Parameter Values in SGD

Stochastic Gradient Descent with Momentum

The Stochastic Gradient Descent with Momentum or SGDM is an extension of the traditional Stochastic Gradient Descent (SGD) algorithm. While SGD is effective due to its computational efficiency, it has the disadvantage of sometimes being erratic in its search for the global minimum. This is where SGDM comes in, providing a more refined approach.

The SGDM incorporates the concept of momentum, which is analogous to a heavy ball rolling through the loss function landscape. Just as a ball gains speed and continues along its path, momentum helps the parameter updates maintain direction and be less perturbed by the "noisy" gradients. This is achieved by combining the gradient of the current batch with the previous gradients, effectively "smoothing" the updates. Incorporating momentum allows the algorithm to dampen oscillations and converge more quickly and smoothly.

In SGDM, instead of calculating the gradient based solely on the current batch, the algorithm keeps track of past gradients and adds a fraction of them to the current gradient. This fraction is controlled by a parameter often referred to as γ(gamma), which typically has a value such as 0.9. This means that 90% of the update from the previous step is added to the current step, providing the algorithm with a memory of past updates and thus a smoother trajectory towards the minimum.

Summary

This chapter explains that gradient descent is an essential algorithm in machine learning that minimizes the loss function, much like a blindfolded person using the slope of a mountain to find the lowest point. It describes how this algorithm iteratively adjusts model parameters to minimize the difference between predicted and actual results, using a learning rate to control the step size. The chapter illustrates this with an example where a linear equation is fitted to a two-dimensional data set by iteratively adjusting parameters 'a' and 'b', resulting in a reduction in loss over time, as visualized in the accompanying graphs. In addition, the text introduces Stochastic Gradient Descent (SGD) as an efficient alternative for large datasets, where model parameter updates are made using a random subset of the data, called a batch. SGD with Momentum (SGDM) is also discussed as an extension of SGD that incorporates memory of past updates to smooth the optimization trajectory, using a momentum coefficient to mix past and present gradients. The essence of the chapter is to convey how Gradient Descent and its variants optimize model parameters for more accurate predictions, which is essential in the journey of learning and improvement in AI and machine learning.

Chapter 4: Foundations of Neural Networks

At the core of many AI systems lies the concept of neural networks. These networks, inspired by the human brain's architecture, are designed to learn and make decisions from data. Understanding neural networks is key to comprehending how machines perform tasks ranging from recognizing images to processing language.

This chapter will guide you through the foundational concepts of neural networks, starting from simple building blocks to more complex structures. We will explore how data is represented in AI using tensors, which are multi-dimensional arrays that extend beyond simple scalars and matrices. These structures enable the efficient handling of high-dimensional data, a necessity in machine learning and deep learning applications. We will also delve into the perceptron, a fundamental unit of a neural network, and understand its mechanisms and importance in learning.

The journey from understanding basic neural units to exploring their more complex implementations will equip you with a solid foundation in neural network principles, setting the stage for more advanced topics in AI.

Introduction to Tensors and their significance in AI

Tensors are a fundamental concept in AI and machine learning that can be thought of as multi-dimensional containers for data. Most of us are already familiar with scalars, vectors, and matrices. Tensors can be seen as a generalization that encompasses all these concepts, along with higher-dimensional data structures. They serve as a versatile term to represent various data types and containers, allowing us to work with more complex and multidimensional datasets.

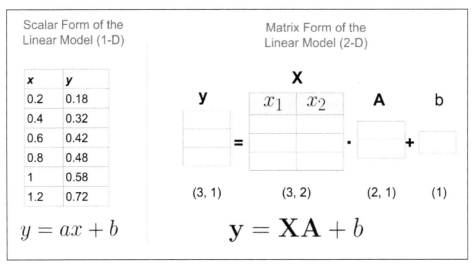

Figure 4.1: Linear regression models: 1-D and 2-D data representations.

The image shows two sections, "1-D" and "2-D," representing one-dimensional and two-dimensional linear regression models. In the "1-D" part, there is a table listing pairs of 'x' and 'y' values, suggesting data points for a simple linear regression. The formula $y=ax+b$ describes the relationship between x and y, with a being the slope and b the y-intercept. The "2-D" section is prepared for two-dimensional data, with a blank table set to include x_1, x_2 and y values. The regression model extends to two predictors, represented by the equation:

$$y = a_1 x_1 + a_2 x_2 + b$$

In this form, x_1 and x_2 are the two input features or independent variables, while a_1 and a_2 are their corresponding weights (slopes). The term b is the bias or intercept. This model allows us to capture the influence of both predictors on the target variable y, enabling more complex relationships to be modeled compared to the single-variable case.

The below matrix equation further translates this model into matrix notation:

$$y = XA + b$$

Here y is the outcome vector, X is the predictor matrix, A is the coefficient matrix, and b is the intercept vector. Their dimensions are indicated as (3, 1) for y, (3, 2) for X, (2, 1) for A, and (1) for b, demonstrating how matrix multiplication will be used to compute y from X and A, with the addition of

b.

Tensor examples

Tensors are a type of data structure used in linear algebra and are particularly important in various applications, including physics, computer science, and data analysis. They are generalizations of more familiar mathematical entities like scalars, vectors, and matrices to an arbitrary number of dimensions. Below, we will explore the concept of tensors by looking at their different forms, starting from a simple matrix to more complex structures.

2-Dimensional Tensor

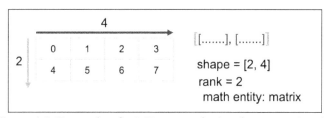

Figure 4.2: Example of a 2-D tensor depicted as a matrix with dimensions 2x4

A matrix is the simplest form of a tensor, essentially a 2-dimensional array. Consider a matrix with a shape of [2, 4], which means it has 2 rows and 4 columns. This matrix is a rectangular grid filled with numbers, such as integers from 0 to 7. In linear algebra, this matrix is known as a 2nd-rank tensor due to its two dimensions, requiring two indices to identify any individual element.

In the above diagram we have used the darker arrow (left-to-right) and the inner square brackets to indicate the column dimension which is 4 in the 2-D tensor example. Similarly, we have used the lighter arrow (top-down) and external square brackets to signify the row dimension which is 2 in the above example.

3-Dimensional Tensor

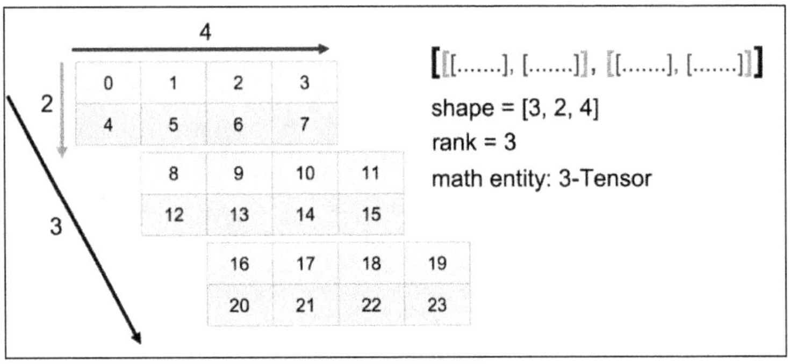

Figure 4.3: A 3-D tensor visualized as a stack of matrices with shape [3, 2, 4]

Expanding upon the 2-dimensional tensor, a 3-dimensional tensor can be visualized as a stack of matrices. With a shape denoted by [3, 2, 4], it consists of 3 layers where each layer is a 2x4 matrix. This structure is referred to as a 3rd-rank tensor since it requires three indices to locate a particular element within the tensor. In this tensor, the numbers are filled sequentially, creating a block of numbers from 0 to 23, extending our grid into the third dimension.

Please note that we have used a diagonal arrow and external most square bracket to denote the third dimension in a 3-dimensional tensor, which has the value of 3 in the above example.

4-Dimensional Tensor

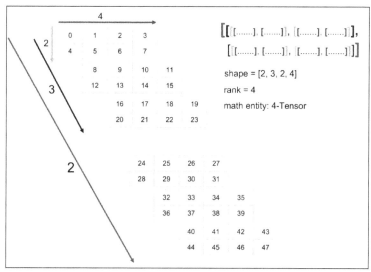

Figure 4.4: Visualization of a 4-D tensor with shape [2, 3, 2, 4]

Progressing to even higher dimensions, a 4-dimensional tensor has a shape of [2, 3, 2, 4]. This structure can be thought of as a list of 3-dimensional tensors, with two such lists forming the complete tensor. It contains numbers ranging from 0 to 47, arranged in an abstract four-dimensional space. This tensor is a 4th-rank tensor as four indices are required to specify each element's position.

Creating Tensors from Raw Data

Tensors are the fundamental building blocks of many modern computational frameworks, particularly in the fields of machine learning and data analysis. By definition, a tensor is a generalized n-dimensional array, where 'n' denotes the rank or order of the tensor. The rank of a tensor defines the number of dimensions, referred to as axes, that the tensor has. The power of tensors comes from their ability to model complex relationships and to represent high-dimensional data structures efficiently.

To illustrate the concept of tensors and how they can be constructed from a sequence of raw data, consider the following examples, where a sequence of integers from 0 to 15 serves as our raw data:

Data: 0, 1, 2, 3, 4, 5, 6, 7, 8, 9, 10, 11, 12, 13, 14, 15

Rank 2 Tensor:

When we arrange this sequence into a Rank 2 tensor (akin to a 2D array or matrix), we can define its shape as [2, 8]. This means the tensor has two dimensions: the first dimension has a length of 2, and the second has a length of 8. Such a structure can be used to represent matrices, where the first axis can represent rows and the second columns. The tensor thus contains two arrays, each hosting eight elements of the data sequence. Here is how we can show it in a tensor form:

```
Tensor
  rank: 2
  shape: [2,8]
  values:
   [[0, 1, 2, 3 , 4 , 5 , 6 , 7 ],
    [8, 9, 10, 11, 12, 13, 14, 15]]
```

Figure 4.5: Creating a Rank 2 tensor from a raw sequence of integers

Rank 3 Tensor:

Progressing to a Rank 3 tensor introduces an additional dimension, which can be thought of as a depth. A tensor with a shape of [2, 4, 2] can be imagined as two layers of 2D arrays, each layer containing four rows and two columns. This format is particularly useful for applications like computer vision, where an image might be represented as a tensor with dimensions corresponding to height, width, and color channels. Here is how we can show it in a tensor form:

```
Tensor
  rank: 3
  shape: [2,4,2]
  values:
   [[[0, 1],
     [2, 3],
     [4, 5],
     [6, 7]],
    [[8, 9],
     [10, 11],
     [12, 13],
     [14, 15]]]
```

Figure 4.6: Example of a Rank 3 tensor with shape [2, 4, 2]

Rank 4 Tensor:

A Rank 4 tensor further extends the complexity, now with a shape of [2, 2, 2, 2]. It can be visualized as a list of Rank 3 tensors, or a 4-dimensional grid. Each 'slice' of this tensor adds another layer of depth to the data structure, allowing it to represent even more complex associations such as time-series data within a spatial framework, which could be used in video processing or high-dimensional scientific computations. Here is how we can show it in a tensor form:

```
Tensor
  rank: 4
  shape: [2,2,2,2]
  values:
    [[[[0, 1],
      [2, 3]],
     [[4, 5],
      [6, 7]]],
    [[[8, 9],
      [10, 11]],
     [[12, 13],
      [14, 15]]]]
```

Figure 4.7: A Rank 4 tensor with shape [2, 2, 2, 2]

Tensors provide a multi-dimensional framework that can scale from simple lists (1D tensors) to matrices (2D tensors) and beyond. As we have seen with the raw data example ranging from Rank 2 to Rank 4 tensors, their ability to encapsulate higher dimensions allows us to handle complex, structured data. Understanding how to construct and manipulate tensors is essential for leveraging the full power of high-dimensional data analysis and computational models.

Real-world Tensor examples

In this section we explore and discuss various real-world examples of tensors of different ranks and their respective shapes, along with visual representations to illustrate how they are structured.

Rank 2 Tensor Example: Insurance Risk Data

In this example the insurance risk data is structured within a tensor of rank 2.

It encapsulates key features—age, zip code, and income. Visually interpreted through a bar graph, each bar signifies an individual sample's data point. The data is arranged in a 2-dimensional array form, with its shape designated as [4, 3], corresponding to the four samples across three feature columns.

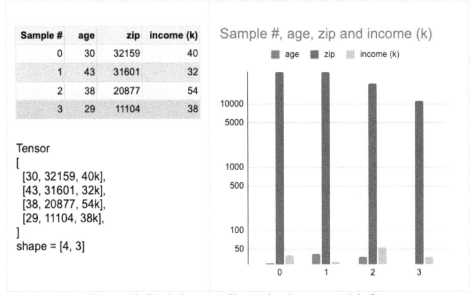

Figure 4.8: Rank 2 tensor illustrating insurance risk data

Rank 3 Tensor Example: Stock Prices Data

In this example, we observe a Rank 3 tensor that serves to encapsulate stock prices data, detailing features such as Open, High, Low, and Close prices over a series of time steps. The tensor is organized into two distinct blocks, each containing six sequences that represent the time steps, along with four specific features associated with stock price movements. A line graph is provided for visual interpretation, illustrating the fluctuations in stock prices over time per feature. The shape of the tensor is precisely [2, 6, 4], reflecting the two samples, six time steps, and four features within the dataset.

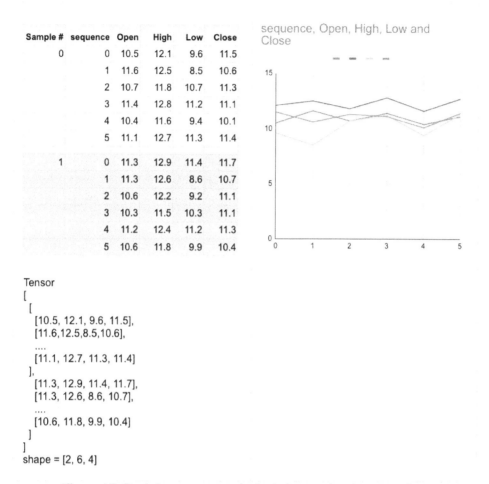

Sample #	sequence	Open	High	Low	Close
0	0	10.5	12.1	9.6	11.5
	1	11.6	12.5	8.5	10.6
	2	10.7	11.8	10.7	11.3
	3	11.4	12.8	11.2	11.1
	4	10.4	11.6	9.4	10.1
	5	11.1	12.7	11.3	11.4
1	0	11.3	12.9	11.4	11.7
	1	11.3	12.6	8.6	10.7
	2	10.6	12.2	9.2	11.1
	3	10.3	11.5	10.3	11.1
	4	11.2	12.4	11.2	11.3
	5	10.6	11.8	9.9	10.4

```
Tensor
[
 [
  [10.5, 12.1, 9.6, 11.5],
  [11.6,12.5,8.5,10.6],
  ....
  [11.1, 12.7, 11.3, 11.4]
 ],
  [11.3, 12.9, 11.4, 11.7],
  [11.3, 12.6, 8.6, 10.7],
  ....
  [10.6, 11.8, 9.9, 10.4]
 ]
]
shape = [2, 6, 4]
```

Figure 4.9: Rank 3 tensor example depicting stock prices over time

Rank 4 Tensor Example: Image Data

In this example (Figure 4.10), the Rank 4 tensor is tailored for handling image data, showcasing two separate 2x2 pixel images with color encoding via Red, Green, and Blue (RGB) channels. The visual portion of the display consists of two groups of colored squares, each mirroring the pixel values stored within the tensor. The defined tensor shape [2, 2, 2, 3] reveals the dataset's structure: 2 samples, each one a 2x2 image in terms of height and width, and 3 distinct channels corresponding to the color depth for RGB.

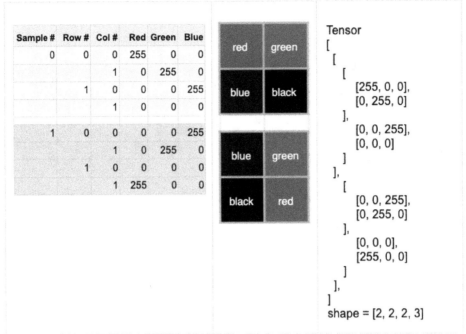

Sample #	Row #	Col #	Red	Green	Blue
0	0	0	255	0	0
		1	0	255	0
	1	0	0	0	255
		1	0	0	0
1	0	0	0	0	255
		1	0	255	0
	1	0	0	0	0
		1	255	0	0

```
Tensor
[
  [
    [
      [255, 0, 0],
      [0, 255, 0]
    ],
      [0, 0, 255],
      [0, 0, 0]
    ]
  ],
  [
      [0, 0, 255],
      [0, 255, 0]
    ],
      [0, 0, 0],
      [255, 0, 0]
    ]
  ],
]
shape = [2, 2, 2, 3]
```

Figure 4.10: A Rank 4 tensor example visualizing 2x2 pixel images with RGB channels

The Perceptron: Building block of AI

A perceptron is a fundamental building block of artificial intelligence and machine learning. Think of it as a simplified model of a neuron in our brain. It takes inputs, multiplies them by their respective weights, adds them up, and applies a threshold to determine its output. This output is then compared to the desired output, and the perceptron adjusts its weights using a process called gradient descent to minimize the difference between the actual and desired outputs. In essence, the perceptron learns from data to make predictions or classify new examples, just as we learn from examples to make decisions in our daily lives. It's an important concept in AI and machine learning, and it's the foundation for more complex models. The concept of threshold that we talked about earlier is also known as the activation function. The activation function is a mathematical function that takes the weighted sum of the inputs and applies a transformation to produce the output of the perceptron. The threshold can be thought of as a specific value of the activation function that determines when the perceptron should "fire" or produce an output.

To explain Perceptron, a simple activation function such as a step function can be used. The step function compares the weighted sum of the inputs to the threshold. If the sum is greater than or equal to the threshold, the activation function outputs 1. Otherwise, it outputs 0.

Understanding the Perceptron Through Logic Gates

Logic gates are the simplest forms of perceptrons and are essential to understanding how neural networks work. These gates process inputs to produce a binary output based on specific rules - like decision making. By studying logic gates such as AND and OR with different activation functions, we can elucidate the operating mechanics of a perceptron.

AND Gate with Step Function

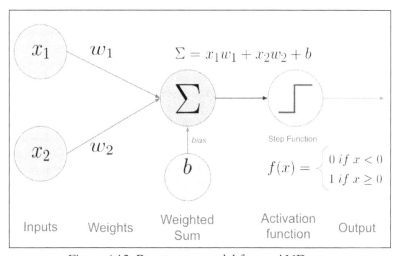

Figure 4.12: Perceptron model for an AND gate

As depicted in the above diagram, the perceptron consists of several key components:

- **Inputs (x_1 and x_2)**: These represent the feature data that we feed into the perceptron. Each input is associated with a weight which signifies its relative importance.

- **Weights (w_1 and w_2)**: Weights are applied to the inputs and express the strength of the connection between the input and the neuron. The perceptron learns by adjusting these weights based on the error of its predictions.

- **Weighted Sum (Σ)**: The below formula calculates the weighted sum, which is the linear combination of the inputs and their respective weights, adjusted by a bias term.

$$\Sigma = x_1 w_1 + x_2 w_2 + b$$

- **Bias (b)**: The bias is a constant value added to the result of the weighted inputs. Think of it like a way to shift the output of the model up or down, helping it make better decisions even when all input values are zero. It allows the model to fit the data more accurately.

- **Activation Function**: The step function used in the perceptron model is defined as:

$$f(x) = \begin{cases} 0, & \text{if } x < 0 \\ 1, & \text{if } x \geq 0 \end{cases}$$

This function activates the neuron (outputs a 1) if the weighted sum is greater than or equal to zero, and deactivates it (outputs a 0) otherwise.

- **Output**: The final binary result of the perceptron's processing, determined by the activation function.

Example Calculations:

In the below table, we see the perceptron in action with specific weights and bias:

- Weights are set as $w_1 = 0.6$ and $w_2 = 0.5$

- The bias is set as $b = -0.8$

		$w_1 = 0.6$ $\qquad$ $w_2 = 0.5$ $\qquad$ $b = -0.8$	
x_1	x_2	Σ	output
0	0	-0.8	0
0	1	-0.3	0
1	0	-0.2	0
1	1	0.3	1

Figure 4.13: Table showing weighted sums and outputs.

The table displays how different combinations of input values x_1 and x_2 affect the weighted sum and the resulting output after applying the step function. For instance, when both x_1 and x_2 are 1, the weighted sum is 1 times 0.6 + 1 times 0.5 - 0.8 = 0.3. Since the sum is greater than 0, the output is 1.

The perceptron's simplicity belies its power. By adjusting weights and biases during the training process, a perceptron can make complex decisions by finding the right balance to correctly map inputs to the desired output. This section has illustrated the basic computations and operations within a single perceptron. Subsequent sections will build upon this knowledge, demonstrating how multiple perceptrons can be combined into a network to tackle intricate tasks.

OR Gate with Step Function

In contrast, an OR-gate perceptron would output a 1 if any of its inputs were true. This behavior can also be explored by adjusting the weights and bias and following the same process as with the AND gate.

Transition to Sigmoid Activation

In the previous section, we discussed the architecture of a basic neural network model, using the step function as our activation function. Now, we will delve into a more advanced and commonly used activation function known as the Sigmoid function.

The Sigmoid function, often represented by the symbol σ(x), is a mathematical function that has a characteristic "S"-shaped curve or sigmoid curve. This function is widely utilized in the field of machine learning, particularly in the context of neural networks.

The Sigmoid function maps any input value to a value between 0 and 1, making it an ideal activation function for binary classification problems, where the output is required to be a probability value. The function's equation is given by:

$$f(x) = \frac{1}{1+e^{-x}}$$

where:

- e is the base of the natural logarithm,
- x is the input to the function.

The Sigmoid function provides a smooth gradient and is differentiable at every point, which is an essential property that allows for efficient backpropagation during the neural network training process.

AND Gate with Sigmoid Function

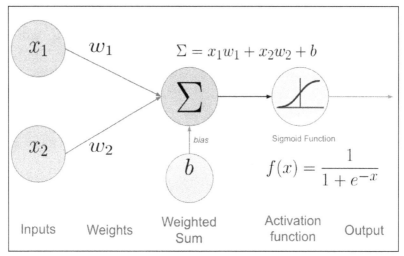

Figure 4.14: Sigmoid activation function applied to an AND gate perceptron

As shown in the above diagram, to calculate the output, we first compute the weighted sum of the inputs plus a bias term using the below equation:

$$\Sigma = x_1 w_1 + x_2 w_2 + b$$

The bias allows us to shift the activation function to the left or right, which is critical for learning complex patterns. Once we have the weighted sum, we apply the Sigmoid function to this sum to get the neuron's output.

Example Calculations:

Let's consider an example where we have two inputs to our Sigmoid based Perceptron x_1 and x_2, with respective weights $w_1 = 5.470$, $w_2 = 5.470$, and $b = -8.30$. A table illustrates the output of our neuron for all combinations of binary inputs (0 or 1) is shown below:

$$w_1 = 5.470 \qquad w_2 = 5.470 \qquad b = -8.307$$

x_1	x_2	Σ	output
0	0	-8.307	0
0	1	-2.837	0.055
1	0	-2.837	0.055
1	1	2.633	0.933

Figure 4.15: Table of weighted sums and probabilities

As seen in the table, when both inputs are 0, the weighted sum is simply the bias b, which after being passed through the Sigmoid function gives an output close to 0. Conversely, when both inputs are 1, the sum is positive, and the output is close to 1, indicating a high probability scenario.

Through these simple but illustrative examples, we gain insight into the role of the perceptron as a building block in neural networks. The perceptron's ability to perform logical operations with different activation functions demonstrates its flexibility and power. The step function provides binary decisions reminiscent of traditional digital circuits, while the sigmoid function introduces the nuance and complexity needed to model more complex, continuous responses. Understanding these dynamics is critical to appreciating the broader capabilities and applications of neural networks in AI.

Summary

Chapter 4 serves as an introduction to the basic concepts of neural networks, emphasizing the role of tensors as central multidimensional arrays for handling machine learning data, from simple scalars to complex high-dimensional datasets. It walks through their use in linear regression, showing how to represent and process data using vectors and matrices. The chapter also covers the practicalities of converting raw data into structured tensors, using real-world examples such as insurance and stock market figures to demonstrate how they can be visualized. In addition, it introduces the perceptron - a core component of AI, like a neuron, that adjusts its weights to improve accuracy - and details its structure and function, including different activation mechanisms. This lays the foundation for understanding the complex functions and learning processes within AI systems.

Chapter 5: Advanced Neural Network Techniques

Advanced Neural Network Techniques serve as a gateway to understanding the sophisticated algorithms that make artificial intelligence possible. We begin with backpropagation, an essential two-step process that iterates between forward data propagation and meticulous backward adjustments to minimize prediction errors. We then shift our focus to multi-layer neural networks, which consist of multiple layers of neurons capable of recognizing complex patterns. These networks refine their predictive capabilities through continuous weight adjustments orchestrated by backpropagation, allowing them to tackle complicated problems with increasing accuracy. Taken together, these sections provide a comprehensive overview of the advanced methods that underlie the learning and adaptability of modern neural networks.

Backpropagation: The backbone of neural network training

Backpropagation is a fundamental technique used in training neural networks to learn from data. It involves a two-step process: forward propagation and backward propagation. During forward propagation, inputs are passed through the network, and the activations of each neuron are calculated using the specified activation function, such as the sigmoid function. The output of the network is compared to the desired output using a cost or loss function. In the second step, backward propagation, the network adjusts its weights and biases by computing the gradient of the loss function with respect to each weight and bias in the network using partial differentiation. This gradient is then used to update the weights and biases using an optimization algorithm, typically gradient descent. By iteratively repeating this process on a training data set, backpropagation allows the network to adjust its parameters and minimize error, effectively learning the underlying patterns and improving its predictive capabilities.

Let's try to depict the backpropagation in a network diagram as shown below.

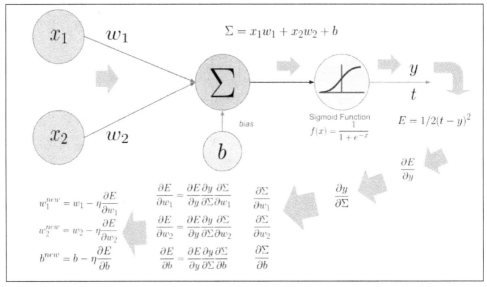

Figure 5.1: Visualizing the backpropagation process in a neural network

This diagram is instrumental in visualizing the backpropagation algorithm—a fundamental process enabling neural networks to learn from data. It represents a microcosm of the neural network's operation, showcasing the flow of data from inputs to outputs and the subsequent adjustment of weights and biases through calculated gradients.

The diagram illustrates a neural network with two inputs (x_1 and x_2), each connected to a neuron by weights (w_1 and w_2). These weights are the adjustable parameters that the network will fine-tune during training. The neuron also has a bias (b), depicted as a separate node, which allows the model to fit the data better by providing an additional degree of freedom. As the inputs are fed into the network, they are first combined into a weighted sum (Σ), representing the neuron's net input. This sum is then processed by a sigmoid activation function, which converts the linear input into a non-linear output (y). The sigmoid function is crucial for enabling the network to capture and model complex, non-linear relationships in the data.

The rightmost part of the diagram captures the output of the network (y), compared against the target or expected value (t), with the discrepancy quantified by a mean squared error function (E). This error measure is reflective of the network's performance; the goal of training is to minimize this error.

Arrows pointing backward from the error (E) represent the backward propagation of this error signal. By taking the partial derivatives of the error with respect to the output ($\partial y / \partial E$) we can measure how much the error changes when the predicted output changes. This tells the network in which direction and how strongly the output is influencing the overall error. Then, by applying the chain rule to relate this back to the weights and bias, the network calculates how to adjust $\mathbf{w_1}$, $\mathbf{w_2}$, and $\mathbf{b}$ to reduce $\mathbf{E}$. These adjustments are made in the opposite direction of the gradient, hence the term 'gradient descent.

Below are the main steps involved in performing the Forward Propagation and Backward Propagation.

Forward Propagation

The journey of data through the neural network starts with forward propagation, where inputs are passed to the network and processed sequentially from one layer to the next. Each neuron receives inputs, multiplies them by their respective weights, and then adds a bias term. This calculation is the weighted sum, denoted as Σ, and can be expressed mathematically as:

$$\Sigma = x_1 w_1 + x_2 w_2 + b$$

The weighted sum is then transformed by an activation function, which introduces non-linearity into the model, allowing it to learn and represent more complex patterns. In our example, the sigmoid function is used, defined as:

$$f(x) = \frac{1}{1+e^{-x}}$$

Applied to the weighted sum, the output of the neuron, denoted as y, is:

$$y = \frac{1}{1+e^{-\Sigma}}$$

This activation output is what the network uses to make predictions or decisions based on the input it received.

Chapter 5: Advanced Neural Network Techniques

Error Calculation and Backward Propagation

Once the network has produced an output, it must be evaluated to determine its accuracy. This is done by comparing the output y with the target value t, using a cost function, such as the mean squared error (MSE), to quantify the error of the prediction:

$$E = \tfrac{1}{2}(t - y)^2$$

Please note that this equation and the following equations represent the computation for a single training example. That's why there are no summation symbols or indexed variables—those are introduced when extending the calculation to the entire dataset.

The backpropagation phase starts by computing the gradient of this error with respect to the output of the network. This gradient, $\partial y/\partial E$, indicates the direction and magnitude by which the error will increase or decrease with respect to a change in the output:

$$\frac{\partial E}{\partial y} = -(t - y)$$

The gradient is then propagated back through the network, which requires computing the derivative of the output y with respect to the weighted sum Σ for the sigmoid function:

$$\frac{\partial y}{\partial \Sigma} = y \cdot (1 - y)$$

The above equation is derived as below:

$$y = \frac{1}{1 + e^{-\Sigma}}$$

$$\frac{d}{d\Sigma}\left(\frac{1}{1+e^{-\Sigma}}\right) = \frac{e^{-\Sigma}}{(1+e^{-\Sigma})^2}$$

Again:

$$y = \frac{1}{1+e^{-\Sigma}}$$

$$1 - y = 1 - \frac{1}{1+e^{-\Sigma}}$$

$$= \frac{(1+e^{-\Sigma}) - 1}{1+e^{-\Sigma}} = \frac{e^{-\Sigma}}{1+e^{-\Sigma}}$$

Hence

$$\frac{dy}{d\Sigma} = y(1-y)$$

This derivative reflects how changes in the weighted sum would affect the neuron's output after the activation function is applied.

Updating the Weights and Bias

The goal of backpropagation is to use the error gradient to update the weights and bias in such a way that the error is reduced in subsequent iterations. The weights are updated by subtracting the product of the learning rate η and the gradient with respect to each weight:

$$w_1^{new} = w_1 - \eta\frac{\partial E}{\partial w_1}$$

$$w_2^{new} = w_2 - \eta \frac{\partial E}{\partial w_2}$$

Similarly, the bias is updated by:

$$b^{new} = b - \eta \frac{\partial E}{\partial b}$$

To compute the gradients for the weights and bias, the chain rule is employed:

$$\frac{\partial E}{\partial w_1} = \frac{\partial E}{\partial y} \frac{\partial y}{\partial \Sigma} \frac{\partial \Sigma}{\partial w_1}$$

$$\frac{\partial E}{\partial w_2} = \frac{\partial E}{\partial y} \frac{\partial y}{\partial \Sigma} \frac{\partial \Sigma}{\partial w_2}$$

$$\frac{\partial E}{\partial b} = \frac{\partial E}{\partial y} \frac{\partial y}{\partial \Sigma} \frac{\partial \Sigma}{\partial b}$$

The partial derivatives of the weighted sum Σ with respect to the weights and bias are the input values and a constant 1, respectively:

$$\frac{\partial \Sigma}{\partial w_1} = x_1$$

$$\frac{\partial \Sigma}{\partial w_2} = x_2$$

$$\frac{\partial \Sigma}{\partial b} = 1$$

By iteratively applying these updates, the neural network adjusts its parameters to minimize the error, thereby improving its performance and accuracy over time. Through backpropagation, neural networks learn to map inputs to the correct outputs, effectively learning from their experiences.

Multi-Layer Neural Networks and their capabilities

A multilayer neural network is an advanced model used in artificial intelligence and machine learning. Think of it as a collection of interconnected perceptrons, the topic we talked about in a previous session. However, unlike a perceptron, which has only one layer of neurons, a multilayer neural network has multiple layers stacked on top of each other. Each layer receives input from the previous layer and applies a mathematical operation called an activation function, such as the sigmoid function. This allows the network to capture complex relationships between inputs and outputs. To make the network learn, we use backpropagation, a technique that adjusts the weights connecting the neurons based on the error between the predicted and actual output. This adjustment is controlled by gradient descent or other algorithms. Through this iterative process, the network improves its ability to make accurate predictions, ultimately enabling it to solve complex problems.

Forward Propagation

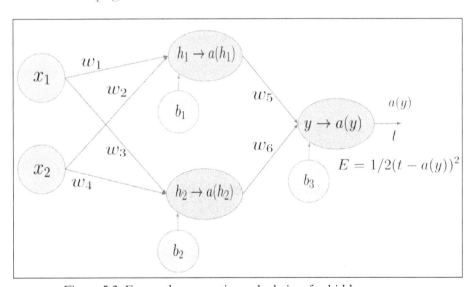

Figure 5.2: Forward propagation calculation for hidden neurons

The first step in forward propagation is to calculate the weighted sum of the inputs and biases for each neuron in the hidden layers. For the first hidden neuron

$$h_1 = w_1 \cdot x_1 + w_2 \cdot x_2 + b_1$$

Where $x1$ and $x2$ are inputs, $w1$ and $w2$ are weights, and $b1$ is the bias for the neuron. The same process applies to $h2$ with its corresponding weights and bias.

$$h_2 = w_3 \cdot x_1 + w_4 \cdot x_2 + b_2$$

The next step is to pass these weighted sums through an activation function $a(\cdot)$, which introduces non-linearity into the model. This is crucial for the network to learn complex patterns. The output of the activation function for the first hidden neuron is:

$$a(h_1) = activation\_function(h_1)$$

And similarly, for $h2$

$$a(h_2) = activation\_function(h_2)$$

The final output of the network, before applying the output activation function, is the weighted sum of the activated hidden neurons (signals) plus the output bias $b3$:

$$y = w_5 \cdot a(h_1) + w_6 \cdot a(h_2) + b_3$$

The output y is then passed through an output activation function $a(\cdot)$ to produce the final prediction $a(y)$. This could be a sigmoid, softmax, or any other activation function depending on the task:

$$a(y) = output\_activation\_function(y)$$

The predicted output $a(y)$ is then compared to the actual target t to calculate the error E, which will be used during backpropagation. Assuming the error as Mean Square Error, can be calculated using the below formula:

$$E = \tfrac{1}{2}(t - y)^2$$

Forward propagation is the essential first step that leads to the generation of predictions in a neural network. It sets the stage for backpropagation, where the network learns from its errors and updates its weights accordingly. Together, these processes allow neural networks to learn from data and improve their predictions over time.

Backpropagation and The Chain Rule

In neural network training, the chain rule is a cornerstone of the backpropagation algorithm, which is used to update the network's weights and biases. This algorithm relies on the chain rule to compute the gradient of the loss function with respect to each weight, allowing the network to learn from data.

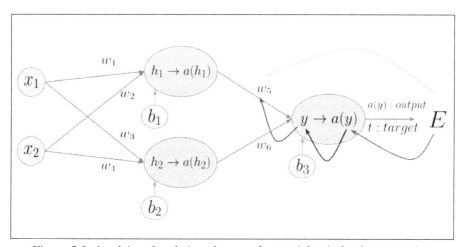

Figure 5.3: Applying the chain rule to update weights in backpropagation

In the above diagram, each neuron's output, such as h1 and h2, is a function of its inputs, which are affected by weights (w1, w2,...) and biases (b1, b2). The final output a(y) is then a function of these neurons' outputs.

To update the weight w5, the chain rule helps us decompose the derivative of the loss E with respect to w5 into a product of simpler derivatives, as shown in the equation above.

$$w_5(\textbf{new}) = w_5 - \eta \frac{\partial E}{\partial w_5}$$

$$\frac{\partial E}{\partial w_5} = \frac{\partial E}{\partial a(y)} \cdot \frac{\partial a(y)}{\partial y} \cdot \frac{\partial y}{\partial w_5}$$

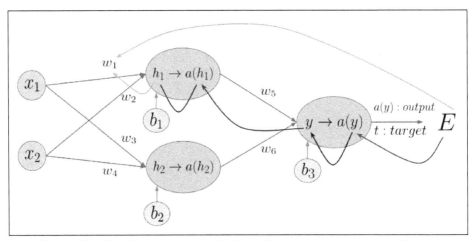

Figure 5.4: Weight gradient calculation using the chain rule across layers

For a weight that is not directly connected to the output, like w1, we must apply the chain rule across multiple layers. The gradient of w1 with respect to the error is computed as shown in the equation below.

$$w_1(\text{new}) = w_1 - \eta\frac{\partial E}{\partial w_1}$$

$$\frac{\partial E}{\partial w_1} = \frac{\partial E}{\partial a(y)} \cdot \frac{\partial a(y)}{\partial y} \cdot \frac{\partial y}{\partial a(h_1)} \cdot \frac{\partial a(h_1)}{\partial h_1} \cdot \frac{\partial h_1}{\partial w_1}$$

Practical Example: XOR Problem

The XOR problem serves as an ideal example to demonstrate a multi-layer network's ability to capture non-linear relationships. For this example, below is our dataset:

x_1	x_2	t
0	0	0
0	1	1
1	0	1
1	1	0

Figure 5.5: XOR dataset used to train the multi-layer neural network

After training the network for a few epochs until the loss (error) is reduced to about 0.01, the various weights and biases become as shown in the below diagram.

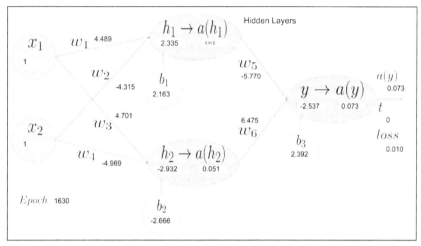

Figure 5.6: Network parameters after training to solve the XOR problem

With these values of network parameters, the predicted outputs are calculated as shown in the below table.

x_1	x_2	Predicted Output
0	0	0.086
0	1	0.858
1	0	0.914
1	1	0.073

Figure 5.7: Predicted outputs of the trained network for the XOR dataset

Multi-layer networks are especially adept at handling complex datasets where the relationship between inputs and outputs is not linearly separable. We will explore the classic XOR problem, where the goal is to classify input pairs based on their exclusivity.

The XOR function outputs true only when the inputs differ. Our dataset is as follows:

x_1	x_2	t
0	0	0
0	1	1
1	0	1
1	1	0

Figure 5.8: Simple multi-layer network
architecture for the XOR problem

A simple MLNN (Multi-layer Neural Network) for the XOR problem consists
of an input layer with two neurons, a hidden layer with two neurons, and an
output layer with one neuron as shown below:

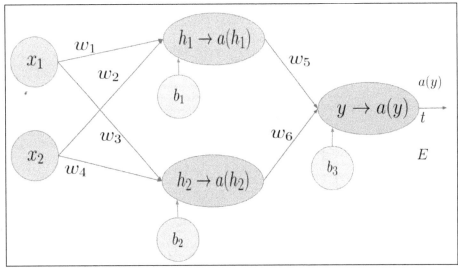

Figure 5.9: Neural Network with Weighted Connections and Biases

Summary

serves as an essential guide to understanding the sophisticated algorithms that make
artificial intelligence possible. It begins with an in-depth exploration of
backpropagation, an indispensable two-step process in neural network training,
consisting of forward data propagation and meticulous backward adjustments to
minimize prediction errors. The chapter then shifts focus to multi-layer neural
networks, comprising multiple layers of neurons capable of recognizing complex
patterns. These networks continuously refine their predictive capabilities through

weight adjustments orchestrated by backpropagation, allowing them to tackle complicated problems with increasing accuracy. This comprehensive overview of advanced methods underlines the learning and adaptability of modern neural networks, presenting both theoretical foundations and practical applications in the realm of artificial intelligence.

Chapter 6: Deep Learning: The Next Frontier

Deep learning is at the forefront of artificial intelligence, ushering in a new era of machines that can learn from experience and understand the world in a way that mimics the human brain. This powerful subset of machine learning has revolutionized fields such as computer vision, natural language processing, and autonomous systems, offering unprecedented accuracy in tasks once thought to be the sole domain of human intelligence.

Introduction to Deep Learning and its applications

Deep learning is a subset of machine learning that focuses on training multi-layer neural networks to automatically learn hierarchical representations of data. By using deep learning techniques such as multi-layer neural networks and backpropagation, complex patterns and relationships within the data can be extracted, enabling the model to make more accurate predictions and decisions. Deep learning has been successfully applied to various fields, including computer vision, natural language processing, and speech recognition, revolutionizing the capabilities of AI systems.

Deep learning frameworks such as TensorFlow, along with other libraries such as PyTorch and Keras, provide a high-level interface and efficient implementation of deep learning algorithms.

Deep learning with a library like TensorFlow involves several steps. First, you need a dataset consisting of input features and corresponding output labels. Then you define your model architecture by specifying the layers, activation functions such as sigmoid, and the connections between them. Next, you build the model by specifying the loss function, optimizer (such as gradient descent), and evaluation metrics. You then train the model by feeding it the training data set for a certain number of epochs, adjusting the weights and biases using backpropagation and gradient descent. During training, the model learns to minimize the loss function, gradually improving its predictions. Finally, once the model is trained, you can use it for prediction by feeding in the inputs and obtaining the predicted outputs. This is done by passing the inputs through the layers of the trained model and extracting the corresponding outputs.

Neural networks consist of layers of interconnected nodes or neurons, which are inspired by the biological neurons in the brain. Each connection can transmit a signal from one neuron to another. The receiving neuron processes the signal and then signals downstream neurons connected to it. Neural networks rely on training data to learn and improve their accuracy over time.

Understanding Deep Learning with TensorFlow

TensorFlow, developed by the Google Brain team, is a profound open-source library for dataflow and differentiable programming across a range of tasks. It is designed to facilitate the development of large-scale neural networks with numerous layers. TensorFlow's high-level API, Keras, has been integrated into TensorFlow itself, making it more accessible to those who may not be experts in machine learning.

TensorFlow excels in its ability to handle deep learning tasks with its static computation graph that allows for efficient performance optimizations. This means that TensorFlow requires the model's structure to be defined in advance before any actual numerical computation occurs. This structure is particularly advantageous when deploying models to production due to TensorFlow's predictability and the ability to optimize for specific hardware.

The provided TensorFlow code exemplifies a simple yet fundamental exercise in neural networks: the XOR classification problem. The XOR (exclusive OR) is a problem that cannot be solved by linear models and requires the neural network to learn a non-linear decision boundary. The code will guide you through defining a sequential model, compiling it with a specific loss function and optimizer, and training it with input data. It also demonstrates how to evaluate the model's performance and make predictions.

As you explore the TensorFlow code, you will learn how to manipulate data, construct models, and use gradient descent to update model weights — all foundational skills for any aspiring data scientist or machine learning engineer. TensorFlow's approach to these tasks is methodical and rooted in a clear structure, mirroring the systematic approach often required in production-level code.

Building a Neural Network for the XOR Problem Using TensorFlow

The XOR problem is a fundamental problem in the field of neural networks. The XOR (exclusive OR) operation returns a true result if the two inputs are not equal and a false result if they are equal. In terms of binary values, where true equals 1 and false equals 0, the XOR operation yields the following results:

0 XOR 0 = 0
0 XOR 1 = 1
1 XOR 0 = 1
1 XOR 1 = 0

This problem is particularly notable because it cannot be solved using a single layer of neurons that perform a linear separation. Instead, it requires a multi-layered network that can capture the non-linearity of the XOR function.

To address the XOR problem using TensorFlow, the following steps outline the process of building, training, and evaluating a neural network model:

Setting up the Environment:

The first step involves setting up the programming environment, which includes importing the TensorFlow library. TensorFlow offers a wide range of tools and libraries that support machine learning and deep learning.

Defining the Dataset:

The dataset for the XOR problem consists of all possible pairs of binary inputs and their corresponding outputs. It is crucial to structure this data correctly so that the neural network can learn from it.

Hyperparameters Selection:

Hyperparameters are the configuration settings used to structure the neural network model. They are not learned from the data but are set prior to the training process. Key hyperparameters include the learning rate, which determines the step size at each iteration while moving toward a minimum of a loss function, and epochs, which define how many times the learning algorithm will work through the entire training dataset.

Model Architecture:

The architecture of a neural network refers to the arrangement of layers and the connections between them. For the XOR problem, a multi-layered perceptron (MLP) with at least one hidden layer is typically used to model the non-linear decision boundary.

Compiling the Model:

After defining the model, it must be compiled. This step involves selecting the optimizer and loss function. The optimizer algorithm will improve upon the weights of the network, and the loss function will measure how well the model is performing.

Training the Model:

Training the model is where the learning happens. The model iterates over the dataset, makes predictions, calculates the error, and improves its weights accordingly.

Evaluating the Model:

Evaluation is the process of determining how effectively the model makes predictions. For the XOR problem, this can be done by comparing the predicted outputs with the true outputs.

Making Predictions:

Once the model is trained and evaluated, it can be used to make predictions on new data. In this case, we're interested in seeing if the model has learned the XOR function.

Output Results:

The final step is to output the results, which includes the input data, the actual outputs, the predicted outputs, and the loss of the model. This information is crucial for verifying the performance of the model.

TensorFlow Code for the XOR Problem

The following Python code snippet provides a practical example of defining, training, and evaluating a neural network to solve the XOR problem using TensorFlow.

```
import tensorflow as tf

# Define input data
X = [[0, 0], [0, 1], [1, 0], [1, 1]]
y = [[0], [1], [1], [0]]

# Define hyperparameters
learning_rate = 0.1
epochs = 500

# Define the model architecture
model = tf.keras.Sequential([
    tf.keras.layers.Dense(4, input_shape=(2,), activation='tanh'),
    tf.keras.layers.Dense(1, activation='sigmoid')
])

# Define the optimizer
optimizer = tf.keras.optimizers.SGD(learning_rate=learning_rate)

# Define the loss
loss = tf.keras.losses.MeanSquaredError()

# Compile the model
model.compile(optimizer=optimizer, loss=loss)

# Train the model
history = model.fit(X, y, epochs=epochs, verbose=0)

# Evaluate the model
loss = model.evaluate(X, y, verbose=0)

# Predict the output
y_pred = model.predict(X)

# Print the output
print("Input: ", X)
print("Actual Output: ", y)
print("Predicted Output: ", y_pred)
print("Loss: ", loss)
```

Let's dissect this code:

- We begin by importing TensorFlow, the library that will allow us to define and manipulate our neural network.
- The **X** and **y** variables hold our input data and the labels (or targets) respectively. For the **XOR** problem, we have a simple set of inputs and corresponding outputs.
- We then define hyperparameters: the **learning_rate**, which controls the size of the steps we take during optimization, and epochs, the number of times the learning algorithm will work through the entire training dataset.
- Next, we construct our neural network model. It's a sequential model with two layers: the first with 4 neurons and a **tanh** activation function, and the second with a single neuron with a **sigmoid** activation function, appropriate for binary classification.
- We then instantiate an SGD (Stochastic Gradient Descent) optimizer with our learning rate. SGD is a popular and effective optimization algorithm in neural networks.
- Our loss function is the mean squared error, which measures the average of the squares of the errors—that is, the average squared difference between the estimated values and the actual value.
- The compile method configures the model for training, associating it with its optimizer and loss function.
- The fit method trains the model for a fixed number of epochs (iterations on a dataset), and we set verbose=0 to suppress the output for a cleaner display.
- We evaluate the model with the evaluate method, which returns the loss value & metrics values for the model in test mode.
- We predict the output for our inputs using the predict method.
- Finally, we print our inputs, the actual output, the predicted output, and the loss to observe how well our model performs.

Introduction to Neural Networks with PyTorch

As we venture into the realm of neural networks and deep learning, PyTorch stands out as an intuitive and powerful library for both research prototyping and production deployment. Developed by Facebook's AI Research lab, PyTorch offers dynamic computation graphs that allow for flexibility in building complex architectures. Its eager execution environment ensures that operations are computed as they are called, making debugging and understanding the code easier for developers.

In contrast to TensorFlow's static graph paradigm, PyTorch's dynamic nature allows for more interactive and iterative design and debugging, which can be particularly beneficial for beginners and for tasks that require complex, variable-length computations. Furthermore, PyTorch's API is designed to be as close as possible to the Python programming language, which has garnered it a reputation for having a gentle learning curve.

The following PyTorch code provides a practical example of solving a fundamental problem in neural networks — the XOR classification problem. It demonstrates how to define a neural network for a simple binary classification task, compile the model, train it, and make predictions. The code is commented for clarity, guiding the reader through each step of the process.

As you read through and run the following code, you will gain insights into the typical workflow of a PyTorch project, which involves data preparation, model definition, loss function specification, and the training loop — a sequence of forward passes, backward passes, and weight updates. This hands-on example will solidify your understanding of the core concepts in neural networks and the use of PyTorch as a tool to build them.

PyTorch Code for the XOR Problem

```
import torch
import torch.nn as nn
import torch.optim as optim

# Define input data
X = torch.tensor([[0.0, 0.0], [0.0, 1.0], [1.0, 0.0], [1.0, 1.0]])
y = torch.tensor([[0.0], [1.0], [1.0], [0.0]])

# Define hyperparameters
learning_rate = 0.1
epochs = 500

# Define the model architecture
class XORModel(nn.Module):
    def __init__(self):
        super(XORModel, self).__init__()
        self.layer1 = nn.Linear(2, 4)
```

```
        self.layer2 = nn.Linear(4, 1)
        self.tanh = nn.Tanh()
        self.sigmoid = nn.Sigmoid()

    def forward(self, x):
        x = self.tanh(self.layer1(x))
        x = self.sigmoid(self.layer2(x))
        return x

model = XORModel()

# Define the optimizer
optimizer = optim.SGD(model.parameters(), lr=learning_rate)

# Define the loss
criterion = nn.MSELoss()

# Train the model
for epoch in range(epochs):
    # Forward pass: Compute predicted y by passing x to the model
    y_pred = model(X)

    # Compute and print loss
    loss = criterion(y_pred, y)

    # Zero gradients, perform a backward pass, and update the weights.
    optimizer.zero_grad()
    loss.backward()
    optimizer.step()

# Evaluate the model
model.eval()

with torch.no_grad():
    y_pred = model(X)
    loss = criterion(y_pred, y)

# Print the output
print("Input: ", X.numpy())
print("Actual Output: ", y.numpy())
print("Predicted Output: ", y_pred.numpy())
print("Loss: ", loss.item())
```

Explanation of the PyTorch code:

- We start by importing the necessary PyTorch modules for defining the network (nn), optimizing its weights (optim), and handling the data (torch).

- The input data X and the labels y are defined as tensors, which are the PyTorch equivalent of NumPy arrays and are used to hold input and output data.
- Hyperparameters are defined in the same way as in the TensorFlow example.
- The neural network model is defined as a class **XORModel** that inherits from **nn.Module**. Inside the class, we define the layers and the activation functions. In the **forward** method, we specify how the data flows through the network (forward pass).
- The optimizer is defined as an SGD optimizer, which will update the model's weights. It is given the parameters (weights) of the model to optimize and the learning rate.
- The loss function is defined using the **MSELoss** class, which creates a criterion that measures the mean squared error between the output and the target.
- The training loop involves making predictions (forward pass), calculating the loss, and then updating the model's parameters (backpropagation).
- After training, the model is set to evaluation mode with **model.eval()**, which tells PyTorch that the model is in inference mode, not training mode.
- Finally, we use **torch.no_grad()** to ensure that the operations inside do not track gradients, which is not necessary for evaluation and prediction and saves memory.
- The outputs and the loss are printed to verify the model's performance.

Data requirements for training deep learning models

Data is the fuel that powers the learning process of artificial intelligence models. It serves as the foundation upon which these models are built and trained to recognize patterns, make predictions, and generate meaningful insights. The availability and quality of data directly impact the performance and effectiveness of deep learning algorithms. When training a deep learning model, a large and diverse dataset is crucial to expose the model to a wide range of examples and variations, enabling it to learn robust and generalizable representations. The more data we provide, the better the model can learn and understand complex patterns and relationships in the data. Additionally, the quality of the data matters as it influences the model's ability to generalize well to new, unseen examples.

The subsequent sections will walk you through two distinct examples that illuminate the practical aspects of dataset structure, preparation, and utilization. We'll explore how a relatively simple dataset can teach a model to classify flowers while a more complex dataset can be used to predict real estate prices. These examples will illustrate the importance of data diversity and quality, and how they empower models to make accurate predictions. By examining these datasets, we will gain insights into how to effectively prepare and leverage data for training purposes, setting the stage for our exploration into the world of machine learning through hands-on examples.

Dataset Example: Iris Flower Classification

Introduction

The Iris Flower dataset is a classic in the field of machine learning, offering a straightforward classification challenge. This dataset is essential for beginners to familiarize themselves with the concepts of machine learning. It involves predicting the species of an iris flower based on the measurements of its petals and sepals.

Dataset Overview

- **Dataset Source**: The Iris Flower Dataset can be accessed from the *UCI Machine Learning Repository*, a widely used online resource that hosts a variety of benchmark datasets for machine learning research and experimentation. The Iris dataset, contributed by Ronald A. Fisher in 1936, remains one of the most cited and utilized datasets for introducing classification algorithms.

- **Sample Data**: The dataset contains four features: sepal length, sepal width, petal length, and petal width, and a label for the species of the iris flower, which can be one of three types: Iris-setosa, Iris-versicolor, or Iris-virginica.

Data Representation

SepalLength	SepalWidth	PetalLength	PetalWidth	Species
5.1	3.5	1.4	0.2	Iris-setosa
7.0	3.2	4.7	1.4	Iris-versicolor
6.3	3.3	6.0	2.5	Iris-virginica

This is how the data looks like when downloaded from the dataset source. Each row represents a single flower sample, with the first four columns showing numerical measurements of the flower's sepals and petals, and the last column providing the species label.

Deep Learning Model Architecture

The neural network for this classification task begins with an input layer that takes in the four features.

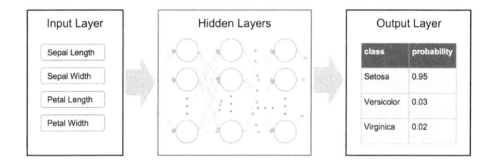

It processes the data through one or more hidden layers and outputs the class probabilities in the output layer. For example, the network might predict a 95% probability for Iris-setosa.

Dataset Example: House Price Prediction

Introduction

The Boston House Prices Dataset provides a more complex scenario, ideal for regression tasks in machine learning. It includes various features such as crime rate, average room number, and more, to predict the median value of homes in different Boston areas.

Dataset Overview

- **Dataset source**: The Boston House Prices Dataset can be accessed through popular platforms such as Kaggle, which host publicly available datasets for machine learning projects. Originally published by the U.S. Census and made available by the UCI Machine Learning Repository, this dataset has become a standard benchmark for regression problems. It contains a variety of features including crime rate, average number of rooms per dwelling, proximity to employment centers, and more. These attributes are used to predict the median value of owner-occupied homes in different suburbs of Boston.

- **Sample Data**: Includes 14 attributes such as crime rate (CRIM), proportion of non-retail business acres per town (INDUS), and others, along with the median value (MEDV) of owner-occupied homes.

Data Representation

CRIM	ZN	INDUS	CHAS	NOX	...	B	LSTAT	MEDV
0.00632	18	2.31	0	0.538	...	396.9	4.98	24
0.02731	0	7.07	0	0.469	...	396.9	9.14	21.6
0.02729	0	7.07	0	0.469	...	392.83	4.03	34.7

This is how the data looks like when downloaded from the dataset source. Each column represents a feature used for prediction, while the last column contains the house prices, which serve as the labels for the model. Some columns have been omitted here for better readability.

Deep Learning Model Architecture

The below diagram illustrates a neural network model designed for house price prediction. The network begins with an input layer containing one neuron for each feature in the dataset. This input is passed through one or more hidden layers, and finally to an output layer that produces a single predicted value the estimated house price.

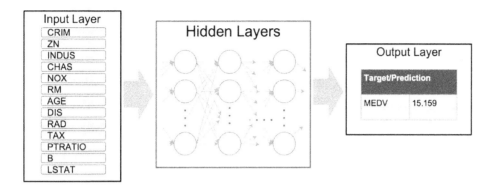

Activation Functions, Optimizers, and Loss Functions in Deep Learning

In the fascinating world of deep learning, the success of neural network models hinges on the intricate interplay of various components, among which activation functions, optimizers, and loss functions are pivotal. This section delves into the nuanced roles and significance of these components, shedding light on how they collectively empower neural networks to learn complex patterns and make intelligent decisions. Activation functions, acting as the heartbeat of neural networks, introduce necessary non-linearity, enabling these networks to capture and model the complex, intricate patterns present in real-world data. From classic sigmoid and tanh functions to modern ReLU and its variants, each activation function has unique characteristics and applications, making their understanding crucial for effective model design. Similarly, optimizers, the navigators of the neural network's learning journey, play a critical role in updating the network's weights and determining the efficiency and speed of the learning process. This section explores various optimizers, from the traditional gradient descent to advanced algorithms like Adam and RMSprop, highlighting how their selection can dramatically influence the learning dynamics and overall performance of deep learning models. Additionally, loss functions act as the guiding compass, providing essential feedback on the model's performance by quantifying the difference between predicted outputs and actual values. Covering a range from mean squared error in regression tasks to cross-entropy in classification challenges, this section emphasizes their pivotal role in guiding the optimization process. By gaining a comprehensive understanding of how these components work individually and synergistically, one can better grasp how to effectively harness their power in the realm of deep learning, leading to more intelligent and capable neural network models.

Activation Functions

An "activation function" is a crucial component of a neural network that helps introduce non-linearity and enables the network to learn complex patterns and relationships in data. Think of it as a mathematical function that takes the weighted sum of inputs from the previous layer and applies a transformation to produce an output for each neuron. It acts as a decision-maker, determining whether the neuron should be activated or not based on the input it receives. Activation functions like the sigmoid function or the rectified linear unit (ReLU) function are commonly used. By applying these functions, the network becomes capable of learning and modeling complicated relationships in the data, enhancing its ability to solve complex problems and make accurate predictions.

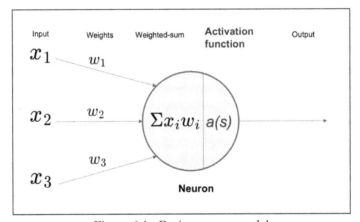

Figure 6.1: Basic neuron model

As shown in Figure 6.1, this is a basic neuron and some inputs x_1, x_2, x_3 are fed to it with weights w_1, w_2, w_3. Then, the weighted sum is calculated as $\sum x_i w_i$. Next, we apply the activation function which produced the output. This output is either the final output or fed into the next layer of the network. There are several different activation functions available because different functions have unique properties that make them suitable for specific tasks. Some functions, like the sigmoid function, can squash the input values between 0 and 1, which is helpful for tasks that involve probabilities or binary decisions.

Other functions, like the rectified linear unit (ReLU), are simpler and computationally efficient, making them effective for many tasks.

Before we explore the specifics of some well-known activation function, it's essential to understand why different functions are used in various scenarios. Activation functions are not one-size-fits-all; they are selected based on the specific needs of the neural network and the problem it is designed to solve. The choice of an activation function can significantly impact the performance and learning ability of a neural network. Some functions are better suited for certain types of data and tasks, such as classification or regression, while others excel in different aspects like computational efficiency or the ability to handle non-linear relationships. Understanding the properties and behaviors of each activation function helps in making informed decisions about which one to use in each neural network architecture. This choice is crucial for optimizing the network's performance and ensuring efficient learning during the training process. Below are some commonly used activation functions.

- **Linear Activation Function**: This function maintains the input as is, without applying any transformation. It's useful in situations where we want to preserve the numerical values of the input.
- **Sigmoid Function**: Often used in binary classification problems, the sigmoid function squashes input values into a range between 0 and 1, resembling a probability.
- **Softmax Function**: Extending the concept of the sigmoid function, softmax is used primarily in multi-class classification problems. It converts the outputs into probability distributions, where the sum of all probabilities is 1.
- **Tanh (Hyperbolic Tangent) Function**: Like the sigmoid but with a range from -1 to 1, the tanh function is useful when we want to center the data, maintaining a zero mean.
- **ReLU (Rectified Linear Unit) Function**: Popular in deep learning, ReLU is simple yet effective, converting all negative inputs to zero while maintaining positive inputs as they are.
- **Softplus Function**: This function provides a smooth approximation to the ReLU function. It is differentiable and is used in scenarios where a differentiable approximation of ReLU is needed.

Let's explore some of these activation functions in more detail.

Linear Activation Function

The Linear activation function, illustrated in the provided graph (Figure 6.2), is fundamentally a direct proportionality operator, where the output is a linear transformation of the input. Mathematically, this is represented as $f(x) = w \cdot x + b$ for a single input/output scenario, where x is the input to the neuron, w denotes the weight, and b is the bias. If we set the bias b to zero and assign the weight w a value of 1, the function effectively becomes the identity function $f(x)=x$, indicating that the output is identical to the input. Therefore, an input of 2 yields an output of 2, as the below graph (Figure 6.2) illustrates with a slope of 1.

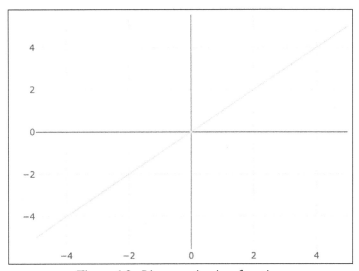

Figure 6.2: Linear activation function

Please note that altering the weight influences the steepness of the function's slope. For instance, if the weight w is adjusted to 2, the relationship between the input and output doubles, making the function $f(x)=2x$. Consequently, an input of 2 will now result in an output of 4, demonstrating that the output is twice the input as shown in the bellow chart.

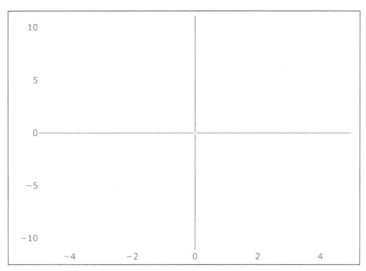

Figure 6.3: Effect of weight change on linear activation

This linear transformation allows the model to scale and shift the input data, providing a fundamental building block in neural networks for tasks where the proportionality of input and output is essential.

Sigmoid Function

In the realm of neural networks, the sigmoid function plays a pivotal role in shaping the curve of decision—a transition from one state to another. Visually represented in the attached graph, the sigmoid function showcases a characteristic 'S'-shaped curve that elegantly transitions from a near-zero value to a value close to one.

Below is the simple form of the sigmoid function:

$$f(x) = \frac{1}{1+e^{-x}}$$

This is a beautiful mathematical representation where the function's output is clearly bounded between 0 and 1, regardless of the input value. This boundedness makes the sigmoid function particularly useful for binary classification tasks, where the output can be interpreted as a probability: the likelihood of the input belonging to one class or the other.

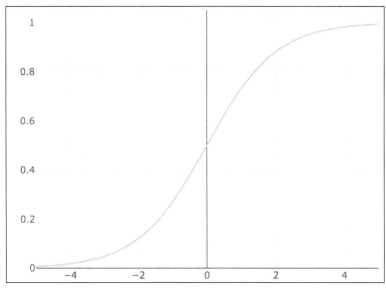
Figure 6.4: Sigmoid function

The sigmoid function serves as a critical transformation in machine learning, converting any real-valued number into a value between 0 and 1, thereby framing it as a probability-like output. Its graph displays an 'S'-shaped curve, which compresses large positive inputs towards 1 and large negative inputs towards 0, ensuring outputs remain within the bounds of a probability range. The central part of the curve, characterized by a steep slope, acts as a sensitive detector of input variations, making it especially useful for binary classification tasks. This region, where the sigmoid function mimics a linear behavior, allows for a clear distinction between outputs, thereby providing a sharp transition from lower to higher probability outcomes.

For a neural network, where decisions are not merely binary, the generalized form of the sigmoid function incorporates weights and biases, adjusting the curve's steepness and position. Below is the generalized form of the equation for Sigmoid function:

$$f(x) = \frac{1}{1+e^{-(w \cdot x + b)}}$$

This allows the function to be more flexible. Here w represents the weighted sum of the inputs, b is the bias, which shifts the curve laterally. This form maintains the same characteristic 'S' shape but enables the function to adapt to the specific data and decision boundaries of the task at hand.

The below table presents the mathematical expressions for some of the most prominent activation functions used in neural networks today, as well as their derivatives. This juxtaposition of functions with their derivatives is more than a reference—it's a map of how neural networks learn and adapt to complex data patterns. Understanding these equations is fundamental for anyone looking to delve into neural network design and the intricacies of machine learning algorithms.

Function	Plot	Equation	Derivative
Linear	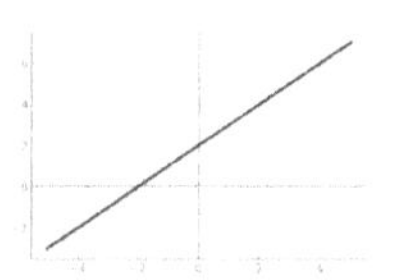	$f(x) = x$	$f'(x) = 1$
Sigmoid	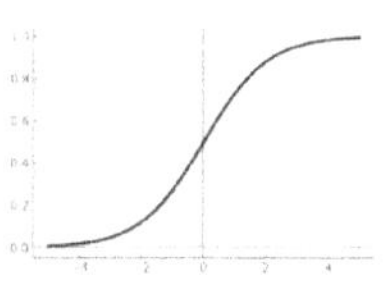	$f(x) = \frac{1}{1+e^{-x}}$	$f'(x) = f(x)(1 - f(x))$
Tanh	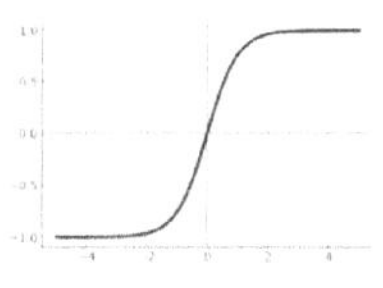	$f(x) = \tanh(x)$	$f'(x) = 1 - \tanh^2(x)$
Relu	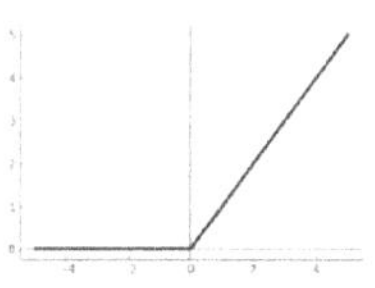	$f(x) = \max(0, x)$	$f'(x) = \begin{cases} 1 & \text{if } x > 0 \\ 0 & \text{if } x \leq 0 \end{cases}$
Softplus	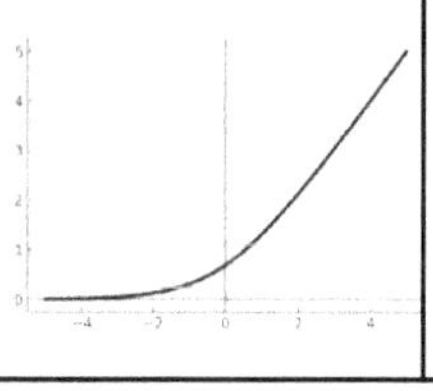	$f(x) = \log(1 + e^x)$	$f'(x) = \frac{1}{1+e^{-x}}$

Figure 6.5: Activation functions and derivatives

Optimizers

Optimizers in machine learning are advanced algorithms that fine-tune the parameters of models to minimize the error in predictions. They are critical in determining the speed and accuracy with which models learn from data. This section will elaborate on the role of optimizers by referencing the foundational concept of gradient descent, as explored in Chapter 3, and will further dissect how these optimizers refine the gradient descent process to achieve efficient convergence.

Role of Optimizers

Optimizers refine the gradient descent process in various ways:

- **Adaptive Step Size**: While gradient descent moves with a fixed step size, optimizers like Adam and RMSProp adjust the step size dynamically. They make it possible to take larger steps when we're far from the goal and smaller steps as we approach the target, preventing overshooting.
- **Momentum**: Just like a ball rolling down a hill gathers momentum, certain optimizers accumulate past gradients. This helps in pushing through noisy gradients and plateaus in the loss landscape, a method used by Momentum and Adam.
- **Stochastic Approach**: SGD, mentioned in Chapter 3, updates parameters more frequently using a random subset of data, which can lead to faster convergence, especially with large datasets.

Importance of Optimizers

The primary importance of optimizers is their impact on the efficiency of convergence:

- **Convergence Speed**: Optimizers can significantly reduce the number of iterations required to reach convergence, translating to faster training times, which is crucial for large-scale applications and complex models.
- **Stability and Accuracy**: By controlling the step sizes and directions, optimizers prevent erratic updates that could lead to divergence or suboptimal convergence, thus enhancing the stability and accuracy of

the model.

- **Practicality**: In real-world scenarios, where data can be noisy and functions non-convex, optimizers ensure that models remain robust and less sensitive to the initial choice of parameters or learning rates.

Stochastic Gradient Descent (SGD)

Stochastic Gradient Descent (SGD) is a powerful optimization algorithm that represents an evolution of the basic gradient descent technique discussed in Chapter 3. While traditional gradient descent updates model parameters using the entire dataset to calculate the gradient of the loss function, SGD introduces randomness into the process, significantly improving efficiency, especially with large datasets.

SGD is predicated on the premise that the gradient of the loss function can be estimated using a randomly selected subset of data, rather than the full dataset. This subset, known as a mini batch, provides a stochastic approximation of the gradient, thus the name Stochastic Gradient Descent.

The core advantage of SGD lies in its use of mini batches. By using a small, randomly selected subset of the data at each iteration, SGD reduces the computational burden significantly. This stochastic approach also confers several benefits:

- *Faster Iterations*: Each update is quicker since it processes less data, allowing the algorithm to take more frequent steps towards the minimum.
- *Noise Reduction*: The randomness helps in avoiding local minima traps, which might hinder convergence in the standard gradient descent.
- *Scalability*: SGD can handle massive datasets that are otherwise infeasible to process with standard gradient descent due to memory constraints.

In each iteration, SGD performs the following steps:

1. Randomly shuffle the dataset at the beginning of each epoch (a full pass through the dataset).
2. Select a mini batch of data points based on a pre-defined batch size.
3. Calculate the gradient of the loss function for that mini batch.

4. Update the model parameters according to the calculated gradient.
5. Repeat steps 2-4 for each mini batch until the entire dataset is processed.

The parameters converge to the optimum as the algorithm processes more mini batches. Unlike batch gradient descent, which might only make one update per epoch, SGD could make as many updates as there are mini batches. This frequent updating enables SGD to converge more quickly in practice, despite the higher variance in the updates.

Below is the fundamental SDG equation, which provides the backbone of the algorithm's operation:

$$\theta_{t+1} = \theta_t - \eta \cdot \nabla L(\theta_t)$$

where

- θ_{t+1} is the parameter vector after the update
- θ_t is the parameter vector before the update
- η is the learning rate
- $\nabla L(\theta_t)$ is the gradient of the loss function with respect to the parameter vector θ_t at iteration t.

In the SGD algorithm the parameters are updated incrementally, guided by a randomly selected subset of data, which is where the 'stochastic' nature of the algorithm derives from.

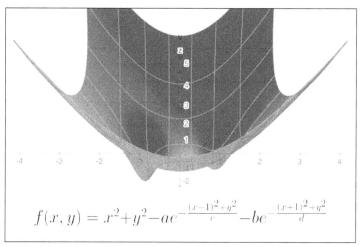

Figure 6.6: SGD loss landscape visualization

To visualize the action of SGD, consider a 3D graph that plots the loss function landscape. The z-axis represents the loss, while the x and y-axes represent the model parameters. The image shows a surface with contours representing different loss values, and the goal of SGD is to find the lowest point on this surface.

The figure below illustrates how stochastic gradient descent (SGD) can navigate the loss landscape toward a global minimum. In this contour map, lighter regions represent lower loss values. The curved lines show the optimization path taken during training. A **global minimum** is the lowest possible point in the entire loss landscape, while **local minima** are lower points in specific regions but not the lowest overall. The goal of SGD is to converge to the global minimum, though depending on the starting point and landscape shape, it may occasionally settle in a local minimum instead.

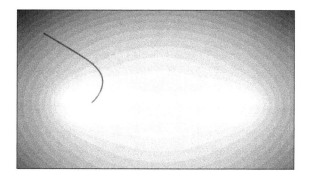

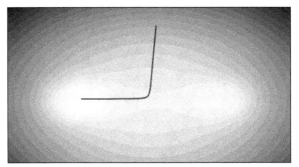

Figure 6.7: Global minimum convergence

Convergence with SGD can be toward a global minimum or a local minimum. A global minimum is the point where the function attains its lowest possible value, ideal for the most accurate model performance. The above images shows the path of SGD as it successfully navigates toward the global minimum, represented by the deepest basin on the graph.

Figure 6.8: Local minimum trap

However, SGD does not always lead to the global minimum; it can sometimes get trapped in a local minimum. The above image represents an instance where SGD converges to a local minimum, which are points where the function value is lower than the surrounding area but not the lowest overall.

Gradient Descent with Momentum (Momentum)

Gradient Descent with Momentum, often abbreviated as Momentum, is a method that accelerates the convergence of the stochastic gradient descent by incorporating the direction of previous gradients into the current update. This technique is especially effective in addressing the oscillations and slow convergence rates that can occur with standard SGD. The Momentum algorithm enhances the standard SGD update rule by adding a fraction of the previous update vector to the current update. This fraction is called the momentum coefficient, and it is typically set between 0 and 1.

In a side-by-side comparison of the convergence plots for standard SGD and SGD with Momentum, one can observe a stark contrast. The plots will reveal that while standard SGD makes progress towards the minimum, its path may zigzag due to gradient variance. In contrast, Momentum's path is smoother and often reaches the minimum in fewer iterations. This comparison highlights the effectiveness of Momentum in navigating the loss landscape more efficiently.

Root Mean Squared Propagation (RMSProp)

Root Mean Squared Propagation, commonly known as RMSProp, is an adaptive learning rate method that addresses some of the inefficiencies of classical stochastic gradient descent. RMSProp modifies the learning rate for each weight individually, often leading to better performance and stability, especially in the context of large-scale neural networks.

RMSProp adjusts the learning rate for each weight by dividing it by a running average of the magnitudes of recent gradients. This means that the update for each weight is scaled by the inverse of the square root of the mean of the squares of recent gradients for that weight.

The key to RMSProp's effectiveness is its ability to modulate the learning rate based on the recent history of gradients. Weights associated with infrequent but large gradients receive a smaller update since the denominator in the RMSProp update rule becomes larger for these weights. Conversely, weights associated with consistent but small gradients receive larger updates. This adaptive process results in a more stable and reliable convergence by preventing drastic changes in the parameter values due to erratic gradients.

Adaptive Moment Estimation (Adam)

Adaptive Moment Estimation, known as Adam, is a sophisticated optimizer that has gained widespread popularity in training deep learning models. It combines the benefits of two other methods: the momentum principle and the adaptive learning rate from RMSProp, to deliver an optimization algorithm that can handle sparse gradients on noisy problems.

Adam's power comes from its two-fold approach: it borrows the idea of momentum by using the moving average of the gradient, which helps in smoothing out the path towards the objective; and it employs the concept of adaptive learning rates from RMSProp, where the learning rate is adjusted based on the recent magnitudes of the gradients. This hybrid approach enables Adam to adjust its learning rate for each parameter based on the history of gradients, making it well-suited for dealing with noisy or sparse gradients.

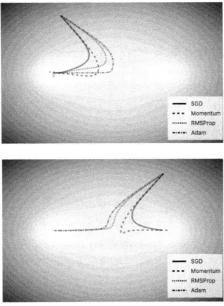

Figure 6.9: Comparing optimization
paths for different algorithms

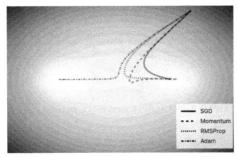

Figure 6.10: Side-by-side visual of SGD,
Momentum, RMSProp, and Adam optimizers

In the quest for the optimal solution within machine learning models, different optimization algorithms can navigate the loss landscape in diverse ways. The above images offer a visual comparison of four such algorithms—Stochastic Gradient Descent (SGD), Momentum (SGDM), RMSProp, and Adaptive Moment Estimation (Adam)—illustrating their paths through a function's contour as they seek to minimize the loss.

When targeting the global minimum (left side of the images), the paths taken by these optimizers highlight their distinctive strategies:

SGD starts with a direct approach towards the global minimum but then veers off, illustrating the challenges it faces with oscillations and potentially getting stuck in suboptimal paths. Momentum accelerates SGD by propelling it across the valleys and over the hills of the loss landscape, providing a smoother and more direct route to the global minimum, as indicated by its path. RMSProp shows an adaptive approach, adjusting its path more responsively to the curvature of the loss function, which helps it stay on course towards the global minimum without the wide arcs seen in SGD and SGDM. Adam combines the strengths of both Momentum and RMSProp, which allows it to navigate the contours with an adaptive, smooth trajectory, often reaching the global minimum more efficiently as depicted by its path.

Loss Functions

Loss functions play a pivotal role in the training of machine learning models. They are mathematical functions that quantify the difference between the predicted values by the model and the actual values in the training data. This difference is commonly known as "loss" or "error." The primary objective of a machine learning algorithm during the training phase is to minimize this loss, which essentially means improving the accuracy of predictions made by the model.

Key Aspects of Loss Functions:

- **Guiding the Learning Process**: Loss functions guide the optimization process in learning algorithms. By calculating the error, they provide a clear objective for the algorithms to achieve - minimizing this error.
- **Quantifying Model Accuracy**: They offer a quantitative measure of model performance. A lower value of the loss function indicates a

model that makes predictions more closely aligned with the actual values.

- **Type Selection**: Different types of loss functions are suitable for different types of machine learning problems, like regression, classification, etc. Choosing the right loss function is crucial for model performance.

Relationship Between Loss Functions and Model Performance

The relationship between loss functions and model performance is a direct and significant one. The choice of a loss function can greatly influence the behavior of the learning algorithm and, consequently, the performance of the model.

- **Convergence to Minima**: Certain loss functions can lead to faster convergence during training, meaning the model reaches its optimal state quicker. This can be especially important in large-scale applications where computational efficiency is a concern.
- **Handling Outliers**: Some loss functions, like Mean Squared Error, are more sensitive to outliers in the data. Others, like Huber Loss, offer a balance between the sensitivity to outliers and convergence properties.
- **Overfitting vs. Underfitting**: The complexity of a loss function can contribute to overfitting or underfitting. Overfitting occurs when a model learns the training data too well, including the noise, while underfitting happens when the model does not capture the underlying pattern in the data.
- **Impact on Probabilistic Interpretation**: Loss functions like Cross-Entropy Loss in classification tasks have a probabilistic interpretation. They not only measure the accuracy but also quantify the certainty of predictions.

As we explore the different loss functions in the following sections, we will delve into their mathematical formulations, practical applications, and the nuances that make each of them unique. This exploration will provide a comprehensive understanding of how these functions shape the landscape of machine learning models.

Mean Square Error (MSE)

Mean Square Error (MSE) is a commonly used loss function for regression problems. It measures the average of the squares of the errors—that is, the average squared difference between the estimated values and the actual value.

The MSE is calculated as:

$$MSE = \frac{1}{n} \sum_{i=1}^{n} (Y_i - \hat{Y}_i)^2$$

Where

- n is the number of observations
- Y_i is the actual value of the observation
- $\hat{Y}_i$ is the predicted value

The squaring of the errors has significant implications: it penalizes larger errors more severely than smaller ones, which can be both advantageous and disadvantageous, depending on the context.

MSE is widely used in linear regression, logistic regression, and other types of regression analyses where a continuous output is predicted. It's particularly useful in scenarios where we need to emphasize larger errors more than smaller ones, as the squaring operation magnifies the errors.

Advantages:

- Sensitivity to Large Errors: Due to the squaring term, MSE is highly sensitive to larger errors. This can be beneficial in cases where avoiding large errors is crucial.
- Differentiability: MSE is smooth and differentiable. This property makes it easy to calculate gradients for optimization algorithms like gradient descent.
- Analytical Convenience: MSE has a simple and convenient mathematical form, which makes it easy to work with analytically.

Limitations:

- Sensitivity to Outliers: The same sensitivity to large errors can become a disadvantage when dealing with outliers, as it can skew the model performance.
- Scale Dependency: The value of MSE is not scale-invariant. It depends

on the scale of the output variable, making comparisons across different datasets or models challenging.

- Mean-Oriented: MSE gives an estimate that minimizes the variance of the errors, which may not always be the desirable property, especially if the distribution of data is not symmetric.

Example Calculation

y	$\hat{y}$	$(y - \hat{y})$	$(y - \hat{y})^2$
3	1	2	4
5	4	1	1
7	7	0	0
9	10	-1	1
11	10	1	1
13	15	-2	4
		MEAN	1.833

Figure 6.11: MSE calculation example

The Mean Square Error (MSE) in the above example is calculated from actual and predicted values. It involves squaring the difference between each actual value (y) and predicted value ($\hat{y}$) to ensure errors are positive, then averaging these squared errors. With the actual values ranging from 3 to 13 and predictions from 1 to 15, the MSE is computed as approximately 1.833, indicating that, on average, the predictions deviate from the actual values by a squared error of 1.833. This metric helps in assessing the accuracy of a predictive model, with a lower MSE indicating a better fit to the observed data.

Mean Absolute Error (MAE)

Man Absolute Error (MAE) is another loss function used to measure accuracy for continuous variables in regression models. Unlike the Mean Square Error, MAE measures the average magnitude of errors in a set of predictions, without considering their direction (positive or negative).

The MAE is calculated as:

$$\mathbf{MAE} = \frac{1}{n} \sum_{i=1}^{n} |Y_i - \hat{Y}_i|$$

Where
- n is the number of observations
- Y_i is the actual value of the observation,
- $\hat{Y}_i$ is the predicted value.

The absolute value of the errors means that all errors are treated equally, regardless of their direction, making MAE less sensitive to outliers compared to MSE.

MAE is widely applied in regression problems where it is important to treat all errors on the same scale. It is particularly beneficial in contexts where outliers are expected but should not significantly influence the model's performance.

Advantages:

- Robustness to Outliers: MAE is less sensitive to outliers than MSE. Outliers will not contribute disproportionately to the total error.
- Interpretability: The MAE is more directly interpretable in terms of average error magnitude, making it easier to explain in layman's terms.
- Equal Weighting: All errors are weighted equally, which can be advantageous when each error contributes equally to the overall model performance.

Limitations:

- Lack of Differentiability: The absolute value function is not differentiable at zero, which can pose problems for certain optimization algorithms that rely on derivatives.
- Scale Sensitivity: Similar to MSE, MAE is also scale-dependent, and hence comparisons across different scales can be misleading.
- No Emphasis on Larger Errors: Since all errors are treated equally, MAE does not emphasize larger errors, which can sometimes be a disadvantage, especially in cases where larger errors are particularly undesirable.

Calculation Example:

y	ŷ	y - ŷ	|y - ŷ|
3	1	2	2
5	4	1	1
7	7	0	0
9	10	-1	1
11	10	1	1
13	15	-2	2
		MEAN	**1.167**

Figure 6.12: MAE calculation example

The Mean Absolute Error (MAE) in the provided example is a measure of the average magnitude of errors between the actual values (y) and the predicted values (ŷ). It is calculated by taking the absolute difference between each actual and predicted value, signifying the average error without considering the direction. With actual values ranging from 3 to 13 and predictions from 1 to 15, the MAE is computed as approximately 1.167. This indicates that, on average, the model's predictions are about 1.167 units away from the actual values. MAE is particularly useful as it gives an even weighting to all errors, providing a straightforward representation of model accuracy without being overly sensitive to outliers.

Huber Loss

The Huber Loss function represents a hybrid approach, incorporating elements from both the Mean Squared Error (MSE) and the Mean Absolute Error (MAE) to create a loss function that is robust to outliers while maintaining sensitivity to small errors. The most salient feature of the Huber Loss is its piecewise definition, characterized by a threshold parameter δ. For errors smaller than δ, the loss is quadratic, which makes it sensitive to small errors, thus driving precise model adjustments during training. For errors larger than δ, the loss becomes linear, which reduces the impact of outliers on the model's updates. This dual nature allows Huber Loss to enjoy the benefits of both MSE and MAE, offering a balanced solution that improves model robustness without sacrificing performance on the majority of the data. The adaptability of Huber Loss to different data distributions by tuning δ makes it a versatile tool for regression problems, particularly when the training dataset contains noisy observations.

The Huber Loss is calculated using the below formula:

$$\text{Huber Loss} = \begin{cases} \frac{1}{2}(y_i - \hat{y}_i)^2 & \text{if } |y_i - \hat{y}_i| \leq \delta \\ \delta|y_i - \hat{y}_i| - \frac{1}{2}\delta^2 & \text{otherwise} \end{cases}$$

The value of δ is chosen based on the specific needs of the problem and the desired sensitivity to outliers. If δ is set very high, the Huber Loss will resemble MSE, and if it is set very low, it will resemble MAE. The choice of δ thus allows for a balance between the robustness of MAE and the sensitivity of MSE.

Calculation Example:

The below calculation is based on δ = 1

y	$\hat{y}$	|y-ŷ|	½(y-ŷ)²	δ(|y-ŷ| - ½δ)	Huber Loss
3	1	2	2.0	1.5	1.5
5	4	1	0.5	0.5	0.5
7	7	0	0.0	-0.5	0.0
9	10	1	0.5	0.5	0.5
11	10	1	0.5	0.5	0.5
13	15	2	2.0	1.5	1.5
				AVG	0.750

Figure 6.13: Huber Loss balancing errors

Below is what each column and row in the above table represents:

- y: the actual values of the observations or targets.

- ŷ: the predicted values generated by the model.

- |y-ŷ|: the absolute difference between the actual and predicted values. It represents the absolute error for each observation.

- $\frac{1}{2}(y-\hat{y})^2$: This is the squared error for each observation, divided by 2. It is used in the Huber Loss calculation for smaller errors (those within the threshold δ).

- $\delta|y-\hat{y}| - \frac{1}{2}\delta^2$: This column is used for larger errors (those exceeding the threshold δ). It calculates a modified version of the absolute error that is less sensitive to outliers. The constant δ is a predefined threshold that determines where the loss function switches from quadratic to linear.

- Huber Loss: This column shows the final Huber Loss for each observation. It applies the quadratic formula for errors less than δ and the linear formula for errors greater than δ. The decision between which formula to use for each observation is based on the value calculated in the previous two columns.

- AVG (Average Huber Loss): The final row under "Huber Loss" is the mean of all the individual Huber Loss values, giving the overall average Huber Loss for the model on the dataset. A lower average indicates better predictive performance with a balanced sensitivity to outliers.

Summary

Chapter 6 is an in-depth exploration of deep learning as a cutting-edge branch of machine learning, with a focus on its revolutionary impact on fields like computer vision and natural language processing. It introduces TensorFlow and PyTorch as key frameworks for building neural networks, detailing the steps from model design to prediction, using the XOR problem as a case study. The chapter underscores the criticality of data quality and diversity for training, illustrated with iris classification and house price prediction examples. It also dissects the roles and interactions of activation functions, optimizers, and loss functions such as sigmoid, ReLU, SGD, Momentum, RMSProp, and Adam, and their influence on model convergence and performance. This chapter serves as a comprehensive guide to the components of deep learning, highlighting their combined importance in advancing AI capabilities.

Chapter 7: Deep Learning Techniques

This chapter ventures into the advanced realm of deep learning, exploring sophisticated techniques and the crucial aspects of managing these complex models. It into the detailed strategies and algorithms that enable deep learning models to perform at their peak, addressing the cutting-edge advancements that are constantly evolving in this dynamic field. Alongside these technical discussions, the chapter also emphasizes the practical aspects of deep learning management, including the efficient storage, loading, and reuse of models. This is crucial for practitioners who need to navigate the practical challenges of deploying and maintaining these sophisticated models in real-world scenarios. By the end of this chapter, readers will have a comprehensive understanding of not only how deep learning techniques are revolutionizing AI but also how to effectively manage these powerful tools in various applications, ensuring their sustainable and efficient use in solving complex problems.

Techniques in Deep Learning and their significance

Deep learning techniques have revolutionized AI, offering solutions to complex problems in various fields. The effectiveness of these techniques lies in their ability to learn hierarchical representations of data, enabling the handling of high-dimensional data with relative ease. Below are the key deep learning techniques and their significance in the field of AI.

Deep Learning Pipeline Stages

The journey of creating a successful deep learning model encompasses several critical stages. Each stage has its unique challenges and requirements, which collectively contribute to the model's final performance and applicability. The typical stages in a deep learning pipeline include data preparation, model design, training, evaluation, and deployment. This comprehensive overview will guide you through each of these stages, highlighting key aspects and best practices.

Data Preparation

Data preparation is a fundamental step in the deep learning pipeline, setting the stage for effective model training and performance. It involves collecting, cleaning, and transforming raw data into a format that can be easily ingested by deep learning models. Below are the key aspects of data preparation, including quality control, augmentation, and preprocessing techniques.

- Quality Data: The foundation of any deep learning model is the data it learns from. High-quality data should be representative, diverse, and substantial enough to capture the complexities of the problem at hand.

- Data Augmentation: This technique involves generating new training samples from existing ones by applying random transformations like rotation, scaling, or cropping. Data augmentation is crucial in preventing overfitting and improving the model's generalization capabilities.

- Preprocessing Techniques: This includes normalization (scaling input variables to a standard range), handling missing values, and encoding categorical variables. Proper preprocessing makes the data more suitable for learning, enabling the deep learning model to converge faster and perform better.

Model Design

Model design is a crucial phase where theoretical concepts are transformed into a practical framework. It's where the blueprint of a deep learning model is drawn, considering various aspects to optimize performance. Below are the critical components of model design, including architectural choices and feature selection.

- Architectural Choices: The architecture of a deep learning model refers to the arrangement of layers and neurons. This includes deciding the number of layers, the type of layers (dense, convolutional, recurrent, etc.), and the number of neurons in each layer. The architecture depends on the complexity of the task and the type of data.

- Feature Selection: Involves choosing the most relevant features from the data that contribute significantly to the prediction task. Effective feature selection can reduce the model's complexity and improve its performance.

Model Training

Model training is the stage where a deep learning model learns from data to make predictions or decisions. It's a process of iterative refinement, essential for the model to capture underlying patterns and relationships in the data. Below are the key aspects of model training, including training methodologies and strategies to avoid overfitting.

- Training Methodologies: Training a deep learning model involves feeding it with data and allowing it to adjust its weights. The choice of datasets, batch size, and sequence of presenting data all play a vital role in how well the model learns.

- Avoiding Overfitting: Overfitting occurs when a model learns the training data too well, including its noise and outliers, and performs poorly on unseen data. Techniques like regularization, dropout, and early stopping are employed to prevent overfitting.

Evaluation and Tuning

The evaluation and tuning stage is critical in assessing a deep learning model's effectiveness and optimizing its performance. It involves a series of steps to measure and enhance the model's ability to make accurate predictions. Below are the essential processes involved in this stage, including evaluation metrics and fine-tuning parameters.

- Evaluation Metrics: Metrics such as accuracy, precision, and recall are used to evaluate a model's performance. The choice of metric depends on the specific problem and the model's intended application.

- Fine-tuning Parameters: Involves adjusting the model's hyperparameters like learning rate, batch size, and architecture to improve performance. This is usually done through a process of experimentation and validation.

Deployment

Deployment is the final, yet crucial phase in the lifecycle of a deep learning model, marking its transition from a theoretical construct to a practical tool. It's where the model is put to the test in real-world scenarios, providing valuable insights and predictions. Below are the fundamental steps and considerations involved in deploying a deep learning model effectively in a production environment.

- Real-world Application: Deploying a deep learning model involves integrating it into a production environment where it can process real-world data and provide predictions.

- Considerations: Deployment considerations include the computational resources required, how the model will receive and process data, and how it will update and maintain over time. Monitoring the model's performance and ensuring it adapts to changes in data or requirements are also crucial.

Modeling Deep Neural Networks: Choosing the Right Architecture

The architecture of a deep neural network is a decisive factor in its success. It shapes how the network processes data and learns from it. Below are the crucial considerations for selecting the most effective architecture for your specific deep neural network.

Network Architecture

Network architecture is a key determinant in the performance of a deep learning model. It defines the model's structure and its ability to process and learn from data. Below are the crucial aspects of network architecture, including the number of layers and units per layer, which need careful consideration to build an effective model.

- Number of Layers: The depth of a network (number of layers) is instrumental in its ability to capture complex patterns. For simpler tasks, fewer layers are sufficient. However, more complex tasks, like image or speech recognition, may require deeper networks. A good starting point is to begin with a simpler model and gradually increase complexity as needed.

- Units per Layer: The number of units (neurons) in each layer should align with the complexity of the function the network is trying to learn. More units provide a higher capacity to learn complex features but also increase the risk of overfitting and computational cost. It's often effective to start with a modest number of units and increase them if the model underfits the training data.

Activation Functions

Activation functions determine the output of a neural network node given an input or set of inputs. They introduce non-linearity into the network, enabling it to learn complex relationships.

- ReLU (Rectified Linear Unit): It is widely used due to its simplicity and efficiency. ReLU activates a node only if the input is above a certain threshold.

- Sigmoid: Commonly used in the output layer for binary classification, as it squashes the output between 0 and 1.

- Tanh (Hyperbolic Tangent): Similar to sigmoid but outputs values between -1 and 1, making it more effective in some cases due to its normalized output.

- Softmax: Primarily used in the output layer of a multi-class classification problem, as it converts logits into probabilities.

Optimizers and Loss Functions

The choice of optimizer and loss function is pivotal in guiding the training of a neural network.

Optimizers: Optimizers are critical components in deep learning that influence how models learn and converge to the minimum of a loss function. They dictate the adjustments to the model's weights based on the data and the loss gradient. Below are the main types of optimizers used in deep learning, including Gradient Descent, Stochastic Gradient Descent, and Adam, each with unique characteristics and applications.

- Gradient Descent: The simplest form, updating weights in the opposite direction of the gradient.

- Stochastic Gradient Descent (SGD): Updates weights using a subset of data, which reduces computation.

- Adam (Adaptive Moment Estimation): Combines the advantages of both AdaGrad and RMSProp by adapting the learning rate based on the first and second moments of the gradients. This makes it more efficient and effective in practice, particularly for problems with noisy or sparse gradients.

Loss Functions: Loss functions are pivotal in guiding the training of deep learning models, quantifying the difference between the model's predictions and the actual data. They play a crucial role in the optimization process, providing a measure for the model's accuracy. Below are the common types of loss functions used in various deep learning tasks.

- Mean Squared Error (MSE): Common in regression tasks, measuring the average of the squares of the errors between actual and predicted values.

- Cross-Entropy: Widely used in classification tasks, especially binary (Binary Cross-Entropy) and multi-class (Categorical Cross-Entropy) problems.

Regularization Techniques: Regularization helps to prevent overfitting, ensuring the model generalizes well to unseen data.

Dropout: Randomly sets a fraction of input units to 0 at each update during training, which helps prevent over-reliance on any one node.

L1/L2 Regularization: Adds a penalty term to the loss function - L1 for the absolute value of weights (leading to feature selection) and L2 for the square of weights (reducing the weight values without making them zero).

Early Stopping: Involves stopping training as soon as the validation error begins to increase, even if the training error continues to decrease.

These tips and tricks serve as a starting point in the complex task of designing and optimizing deep neural networks. The key is to experiment and iteratively refine the model based on the specific requirements of the task at hand.

The Learning Rate and Epochs

Setting the learning rate and the number of epochs are critical in training neural networks, as they directly influence the learning speed and the quality of the model. Below are the guidelines and strategies for optimizing these parameters.

Learning Rate

The learning rate determines the size of the steps the model takes during optimization. Below are the effects of different learning rates and strategies like adaptive learning rates and learning rate scheduling, each with its own impact on the model's training dynamics.

- High Learning Rate: Can cause the model to converge quickly but may overshoot the minimum loss value, leading to unstable training or divergence.

- Low Learning Rate: Ensures more stable and steady convergence but can significantly slow down the training process and may get stuck in local minima.

- Adaptive Learning Rates: Many modern optimizers like Adam or RMSprop automatically adjust the learning rate during training, helping to mitigate some of the challenges associated with setting this hyperparameter.

Epochs

An epoch in neural network training is a complete pass through the entire training dataset. The number of epochs directly impacts the extent to which the model learns from the data.

- Too Few Epochs: The model may underfit, as it doesn't have enough iterations to learn and capture the underlying patterns in the data effectively.

- Too Many Epochs: Can lead to overfitting, where the model learns the training data too well, including its noise and anomalies, and performs poorly on new, unseen data.

Deep Learning Optimization: Strategies and Metrics

Optimization in deep learning involves fine-tuning various aspects of the network to enhance its performance. This includes selecting appropriate learning algorithms, loss functions, and evaluation metrics. Below are the essential strategies and metrics used in deep learning optimization.

Evaluation Metrics

Evaluating the performance of a deep learning network is critical in understanding its efficacy and areas for improvement. Various metrics are used, each serving a different aspect of performance assessment.

- Accuracy: This is the most straightforward metric, calculated as the ratio of correctly predicted observations to the total observations.

- Precision (Positive Predictive Value): The ratio of correctly predicted positive observations to the total predicted positives.

- Recall (Sensitivity): The ratio of correctly predicted positive observations to all observations in the actual class. It's important when the cost of false negatives is high.

- F1-Score: The harmonic mean of precision and recall. It's a useful measure when seeking a balance between precision and recall, especially in uneven class distributions.

Validation Strategies

Validation strategies ensure that a model not only fits the training data well but also generalizes effectively to new, unseen data. Below are key validation strategies.

- Data Splitting: The dataset is split into training, validation, and testing sets. The training set is used to train the model, the validation set to tune the hyperparameters, and the test set to evaluate the model's performance.

- Cross-Validation: Involves dividing the dataset into subsets, and iteratively training the model on some subsets while using the remaining subset for validation.

- Bootstrapping: Another technique where random samples of the dataset are repeatedly selected (with replacement) for training, and the rest for validation. This method is beneficial when the dataset is limited in size.

Best Practices in Deep Neural Networks

Adhering to best practices in designing, training, and deploying deep neural networks help in navigating the complexities of these networks. Below are the key best practices to follow in deep neural network development.

- Data Management: Effective data management is pivotal in the success of deep neural networks. The quality and diversity of data directly impact the model's ability to learn and generalize.

- Data Quality: High-quality data should be accurate, complete, and relevant. This involves meticulous data collection, cleaning, and preprocessing to ensure the data is free from errors and inconsistencies.

- Data Diversity: To avoid biases and ensure robustness, the dataset should represent the diversity of real-world scenarios. This includes variations in demographics, environmental conditions, and other relevant factors.

Model Complexity

Model complexity in deep learning is a double-edged sword that needs careful handling to optimize performance without compromising efficiency. It's a balancing act between creating a model sophisticated enough to capture intricate patterns and ensuring it remains generalizable and computationally feasible. Below are the critical considerations for managing model complexity, including the balance between overfitting and underfitting, computational efficiency, and strategies for simplifying complex models.

- Overfitting vs. Underfitting: Overly complex models may overfit to training data and perform poorly on new data, while overly simple models might underfit and fail to capture important patterns.

- Computational Efficiency: Complex models require more computational resources and time to train. It's essential to balance the model's complexity with available resources and the specific requirements of the task.

- Simplification Strategies: Techniques like pruning (removing unnecessary neurons), using simpler layers, or reducing the dimensionality of the data can help manage complexity.

Experimenting with XOR: A Case Study in Neural Network Configuration and Results Interpretation

In our quest to understand the intricacies of neural networks, the XOR operation presents a classic problem that highlights the necessity of non-linear models. We'll explore an illustrative example to shed light on how different configurations affect the learning process and outcome.

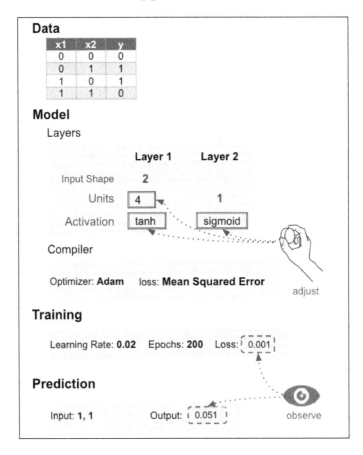

Figure 7.1: Visualizing Data, Model Structure, and Training Progression for Prediction Output

Understanding the XOR Data: The XOR—or exclusive OR—operation is a fundamental logic gate that outputs true only when the inputs differ. For binary values, as shown in our example, the truth table is simple:

- Both 0, 0 and 1, 1 result in 0 (false).
- The combinations 0, 1 and 1, 0 result in 1 (true).

This non-linear separability requires our network to learn from data that cannot be divided by a straight line, presenting an ideal challenge for a small neural network.

Configuring the Model: Our network consists of two layers. The first layer contains 4 units with a tanh activation function, adept at handling negative inputs due to its symmetrical nature around zero. The second layer, a single unit with a sigmoid activation function, provides output in the range (0,1), which is perfect for binary classification tasks. For compiling the model, we've chosen the Adam optimizer for its adaptive learning rate capabilities and Mean Squared Error (MSE) as our loss function to quantify the difference between predicted and actual values.

Training Dynamics: We set our learning rate at 0.02, which is conservative enough to allow gradual learning without skipping over minima. We train our model with 200 epochs or iterations through the full dataset, which in our case is sufficient for the model to learn the XOR function.

Results and Observations: Post-training, we observed that the loss value, which started at a higher value, decreased over epochs, indicating learning and model improvement. The output for the input (1,1) should ideally be 0, as both inputs are the same. Our model's prediction came out to approximately 0.051, which is quite close to the expected value, showcasing the network's capability to grasp the XOR logic.

Comparative Analysis: In a comparative study with various configurations, we observed that increasing the units in the first layer generally decreased the loss and produced a more accurate prediction. However, changing the activation function from *tanh* to *relu* in the first layer increased the loss, suggesting tanh's suitability for this specific problem.

The table provided summarizes multiple configurations with their respective loss and predictions, allowing us to draw insightful conclusions on the network's performance under different conditions.

Learning rate: 0.02   Epoch: 200

Layer 1 Units	Layer 1 Activation	Layer 2 Activation	Loss	Predicted value for input 1,1	Actual value for input 1,1
4	**tanh**	sigmoid	**0.0028**	**0.051**	0
5	tanh	sigmoid	0.0008	0.035	0
6	**tanh**	sigmoid	**0.0006**	**0.499**	0
4	relu	sigmoid	0.1668	0.334	0
5	relu	sigmoid	0.0049	0.062	0
6	**relu**	sigmoid	**0.0017**	**0.038**	0
4	tanh	tanh	0.0083	0.038	0
4	relu	tanh	0.1668	0.334	0

Figure 7.2: Comparison of activation functions and layer configurations

Conclusion: This experiment with the XOR function serves as a practical illustration of how neural network configuration—layer architecture, activation functions, optimizer choice, and training epochs—affects learning and prediction accuracy. It emphasizes the iterative nature of model tuning and the critical analysis required to interpret results effectively.

Managing Models in Deep Learning: Storage, Loading, and Reuse

The world of deep learning is characterized by complex models that require meticulous handling to function optimally. In this intricate ecosystem, the management of these models becomes a cornerstone for success in various AI applications. This importance stems from several key factors:

Efficiency in Resource Utilization: Proper model management ensures optimal use of computational resources. As deep learning models grow in size and complexity, their storage and retrieval need to be handled efficiently to minimize resource consumption and expedite deployment.

Reproducibility and Scalability: Effective model management allows for the reproducibility of results and scalability of AI projects. By standardizing the way models are stored, loaded, and reused, teams can collaborate more effectively, ensuring consistency and reliability in AI-driven projects.

Rapid Deployment and Iteration: In an environment where time-to-market is critical, the ability to quickly load and deploy pre-trained models can significantly accelerate the development cycle. This agility is vital for staying competitive in rapidly evolving AI landscapes.

Facilitation of Transfer Learning: The reuse of models through transfer learning has become a staple in AI. Efficient management of these models enables a more straightforward process of adaptation and fine-tuning for specific tasks, leveraging pre-existing knowledge to achieve better performance with less data.

Deep Learning Model Lifecycle

The below figure depicts the lifecycle of a deep learning model. We begin with training the model on a specific dataset to learn patterns and reduce predictive error. Post-training, the model is validated against unseen data to ensure generalization beyond the training set.

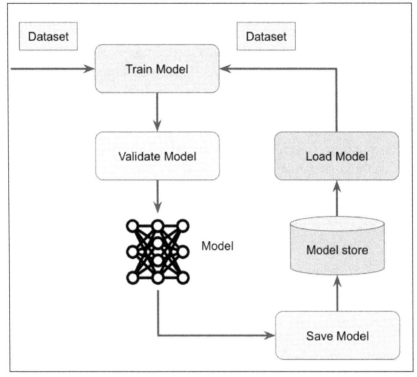

Figure 7.3: Lifecycle stages of a deep learning model from training to deployment

Once validated, the model is stored in a model store, preserving its state for future use. When needed, the model is loaded from the store for further validation, retraining, or deployment in a production environment where it makes real-time predictions.

Storage of Deep Learning Models

Proper storage of deep learning models is critical for their efficient retrieval and reuse. This involves choosing the right storage formats and managing versions effectively. Below are the strategies and considerations for effectively storing deep learning models.

File Formats for Saving Models

The file format for saving machine learning models should be capable of preserving the model's architecture, weights, and training configurations accurately. Below are the commonly used file formats for saving models, including HDF5 and TensorFlow's SavedModel format, each offering unique benefits for model serialization and deployment.

- **HDF5** (Hierarchical Data Format version 5): This is a popular file format used for storing large amounts of data. In the context of deep learning models, HDF5 is beneficial because it can store not only the model weights but also its architecture, and even the training configuration in a single, compressed file. This makes it a comprehensive choice for complete model serialization.

- **SavedModel** Format (TensorFlow's preferred format): This format is specific to TensorFlow and is designed to be easily used in TensorFlow serving. It stores the complete TensorFlow program including weights and computation. It is highly versatile and allows for model versioning, making it ideal for deployment in various environments, including mobile and embedded systems.

- **Pickle** (Python Object Serialization): Pickle is a Python-specific format used for serializing and deserializing Python objects, including machine learning models. It is widely used for saving models trained with libraries like Scikit-learn. Pickle is simple and effective for quick saving and loading within Python environments. However, since it's not language-agnostic and may have security concerns when loading untrusted files, it is best used in controlled settings or for prototyping purposes.

Importance of Version Control in Model Storage

Implementing version control helps in tracking changes over time, managing different versions of models, and ensuring reproducibility of results. Tools like Git, DVC (Data Version Control), and MLflow can be employed for this purpose. They facilitate tracking not only the model's code but also the data used for training and the model's parameters.

Strategies for Efficient Storage of Large Models

Efficient storage of large models involves implementing strategies that optimize space without compromising the integrity and functionality of the models. Below are the effective strategies for the efficient storage of large models, including compression techniques, modular storage, and utilizing cloud storage solutions.

- Compression Techniques: Using data compression algorithms to reduce the size of model files without losing essential information.

- Modular Storage: Storing different components of the model (like architecture, weights, training configuration) separately and loading them as needed.

- Cloud Storage Solutions: Leveraging cloud-based storage services for flexibility and scalability, especially for extremely large models.

Model Serialization Techniques

Model serialization refers to the process of converting a model into a format that can be easily stored or transmitted.

Using Pickle in Python: Pickle is a Python module used for serializing and de-serializing Python object structures. In the context of deep learning models, Pickle can be used to serialize Python objects that define the model and its parameters. Here are some characteristics of this module:

- It's easy to use and can serialize almost any Python object. Pickle is Python-specific, making it convenient for Python-based deep learning projects.

- Pickle is not secure against erroneous or maliciously constructed data. Its use is not recommended for storing models that need to be loaded in different environments or shared externally.

Advantages and Disadvantages of Different Serialization Methods

Different serialization methods in machine learning offer varied advantages and disadvantages, impacting how models are stored, shared, and deployed. Choosing the right method depends on the specific requirements of the task at hand, such as readability, efficiency, and the type of data to be serialized. Below are some key serialization methods along with their respective benefits and limitations.

- JSON/XML for Model Architecture: These formats can be used for serializing the structure of the model. They are human-readable and can be easily edited. However, they are not suitable for storing large binary data like model weights.

- Protocol Buffers: This is a language-neutral, platform-neutral, extensible mechanism for serializing structured data, like Google's protobuf. It's more efficient and faster than JSON/XML but less human-readable.

In conclusion, the choice of serialization method and storage format depends on the specific requirements of the project, including the model's size, the need for human readability, security considerations, and the environment in which the model will be deployed or used.

Model Loading Techniques

The process of loading deep learning models is a crucial step in the deployment and utilization of AI systems. It involves retrieving stored models and preparing them for inference or further training. Here, we discuss the step-by-step process for loading saved models, handling compatibility issues, and optimizing the loading process.

Step-by-Step Process for Loading Saved Models

The process of loading saved models is a essential step in machine learning workflows, enabling the reuse of pre-trained models for predictions, further training, or analysis. It requires attention to detail to ensure the model is correctly reinstated. Below are the steps involved in this process, from identifying the model format and setting up the environment to actually loading and verifying the model.

- Identify the Model Format: Determine the format in which the model has been saved (e.g., HDF5, SavedModel, Pickle).

- Environment Setup: Ensure that the required libraries and dependencies are installed. For instance, loading a TensorFlow model requires the TensorFlow library.

- Load the Model: Use the appropriate function to load the model. For example, TensorFlow models saved in HDF5 can be loaded using tf.keras.models.load_model(filepath).

- Verify the Model: After loading, it's essential to check if the model's architecture and weights are correctly loaded. This can be done by inspecting the model summary or testing it on a known input.

Case Study: Model Management in Action

In this section, we provide a practical example to demonstrate model management through the lifecycle of a simple neural network designed for binary classification. This example will incorporate the images provided to illustrate key points.

We start with a neural network that takes two inputs (x1 and x2) to predict a binary outcome (y). The network is structured with an input layer, one hidden layer with a tanh activation function, and an output layer with a sigmoid activation function, suitable for binary classification tasks. See Figure 7.4 for the network architecture.

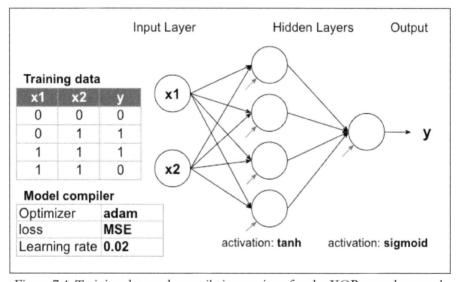

Figure 7.4: Training data and compilation settings for the XOR neural network

Our training data consists of examples with known input-output pairs (see the above figure). The model is compiled using the Adam optimizer with a mean squared error loss function and a learning rate of 0.02 to guide the training process. This figure also provides a snapshot of the model compilation parameters.

118

Once trained, the model is stored for later use. A model summary, as shown in the below figure, provides an overview of the architecture, specifying layers, their output shapes, and the number of parameters.

Model Summary:

Layer (type)	Output shape	Param #
==		
dense_Dense1 (**Dense**)	[null, **4**]	**12**
--		
dense_Dense2 (**Dense**)	[null, **1**]	**5**
==		

Total params: **17**
Trainable params: **17**
Non-trainable params: **0**

Figure 7.5: Summary of the model architecture, including layer details and parameters, generated using *model.summary()* in TensorFlow/Keras

For actual storage, the model configuration is serialized into a JSON object, which includes detailed information on the architecture and settings of the model (see the below figure).

```
{
 "modelTopology": {
  "class_name": "Sequential",
  "config": {
   "name": "sequential_1",
   "layers": [
     {
      "class_name": "Dense",
     "config": {
      "units": 4,
      "activation": "tanh",
      "use_bias": true,
      "kernel_initializer": {
        "class_name": "VarianceScaling",
        "config": { ...
        }
      },
      "bias_initializer": {
```

```
      "class_name": "Zeros",
       "config": {}
      },
      ....
      "name": "dense_Dense1",
      "trainable": true,
      "batch_input_shape": [
       null,
        2
      ],
       "dtype": "float32"
      }
      },
      {
      "class_name": "Dense",
      "config": {
      "units": 1,
      "activation": "sigmoid",
      "use_bias": true,
   }
 ]
}
```

Figure 7.6: Serialized model structure and configuration in JSON format, generated using the model.to_json() statement.

For deployment or further evaluation, the model is loaded from storage. The JSON file is deserialized to reconstruct the model's architecture, and the weights are loaded to restore the trained model state. Should a new task present itself, the existing model can be fine-tuned. By adjusting the weights in the final layer or retraining with new data, the model can be adapted to perform a different but related task. Finally, the model is shared for use by others. Detailed documentation accompanies the model, including the training data used, the architecture, and the training parameters. This information ensures that other researchers or practitioners can reproduce the results or extend the model for their purposes.

Summary

This chapter provides a comprehensive guide on the sophisticated techniques involved in deep learning and the critical aspects of managing these complex models. The chapter begins by explaining the stages of a deep learning pipeline, which includes data preparation, model design, training, evaluation, and deployment. It emphasizes the importance of high-quality, diverse data and discusses various data augmentation and preprocessing techniques. The chapter further delves into architectural choices for model design, the significance of feature selection, and best practices in training methodologies to avoid overfitting. It covers the nuances of evaluation metrics and fine-tuning parameters, as well as considerations for deploying models in real-world applications. The chapter also presents an in-depth discussion on selecting the right architecture for deep neural networks, the role of activation functions like ReLU, sigmoid, tanh, and softmax, and the critical choice of optimizers and loss functions. The latter part of the chapter underscores the iterative nature of model tuning and the critical analysis required to interpret results effectively, using the XOR function as a case study to illustrate the impact of neural network configuration on learning and prediction accuracy. Lastly, the chapter concludes with the best practices in data management, model complexity, continuous learning, updating, and ethical considerations to ensure the development and maintenance of effective, responsible deep neural networks.

Chapter 8: Visual Recognition using Deep Learning

This chapter marks a deep dive into one of the most captivating and fast-evolving areas of artificial intelligence. It unravels the complexities and intricacies of using deep learning for visual recognition tasks, a field where AI has made remarkable strides in recent years. It begins with an insightful look into the use of deep learning for handwritten digit identification, a classic problem that has been a benchmark for the capabilities of neural networks in visual recognition. The chapter then progresses to delve into the nuances of matrix and tensor dynamics, crucial for processing and understanding image data. Furthermore, it provides an in-depth discussion on structuring data for image processing, emphasizing the role of convolution kernels, which are instrumental in feature extraction and image interpretation.

Deep Learning in Handwritten Digit Identification

In the exciting world of deep learning, one of the most fascinating and practical applications is the identification of handwritten digits. This section explores into the intricacies of this application, starting with an introduction to the challenges and significance of handwritten digit recognition. We then explore the MNIST dataset, a cornerstone in the field, which has been instrumental in benchmarking and advancing machine learning techniques. Following this, we examine the role of Convolutional Neural Networks (CNNs) in digit recognition, breaking down their architecture and functionality. Finally, we bring these concepts to life with a case study that guides you through building a handwritten digit recognition model.

Introduction to Handwritten Digit Recognition

Handwritten digit recognition holds substantial practical importance in various fields. It is instrumental in automating processes like postal code sorting, which ensures faster and more efficient mail distribution. In the banking sector, it plays a crucial role in processing bank checks, where recognizing numerical amounts is essential for transaction accuracy. Additionally, in the field of form data entry, digit recognition is vital for converting handwritten forms into digital data, facilitating quicker data processing and reducing manual errors. These applications underscore the need for accurate and efficient handwritten digit recognition systems.

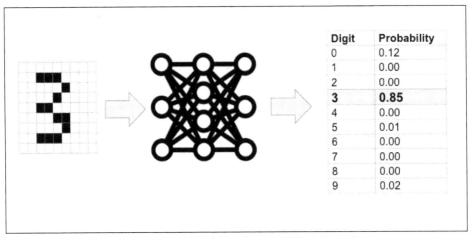

Digit	Probability
0	0.12
1	0.00
2	0.00
3	**0.85**
4	0.00
5	0.01
6	0.00
7	0.00
8	0.00
9	0.02

Figure 8.1: MNIST Handwritten Digit Sample

The journey of digit recognition in the realm of technology and machine learning is a testament to the evolution of AI. Initially, digit recognition was primarily rule-based, relying on predefined patterns and templates. This approach had limited success due to its inflexibility and inability to handle variations in handwriting. The advent of neural networks marked a significant turning point. In the late 20th century, as computational power increased and machine learning algorithms advanced, neural networks began to outperform traditional methods. This shift paved the way for more sophisticated and accurate recognition systems, leveraging the adaptability and learning capabilities of neural networks.

Recognizing handwritten digits presents several challenges. The primary difficulty lies in the inherent variability of human handwriting. Factors such as different handwriting styles, sizes, and orientations create a vast range of variations even for the same digit. Additionally, external factors like the quality of ink and paper, smudges, and varying writing tools add to the complexity. These challenges require a recognition system to be highly adaptable and robust to ensure accuracy across diverse conditions.

The MNIST Dataset

The MNIST dataset, an acronym for Modified National Institute of Standards and Technology, is a large collection of handwritten digits widely used for training and testing in the field of machine learning. It was created by re-mixing the samples from NIST's original datasets. The MNIST dataset contains 70,000 images, each of which is a 28x28 pixel grayscale representation of digits ranging from 0 to 9. These images are split into a training set of 60,000 examples and a test set of 10,000 examples. The simplicity and well-structured format of the MNIST dataset make it an excellent starting point for anyone interested in learning pattern recognition and machine learning techniques. Its manageable size and preprocessed format reduce the need for extensive data cleaning, allowing learners and practitioners to focus directly on building and testing models using real-world data.

Figure 8.2: MNIST Dataset Overview

MNIST has been extensively used as a benchmark dataset in machine learning. It offers a straightforward way to evaluate and compare the performance of various algorithms in accurately classifying handwritten digits. Over the years, it has helped in assessing the effectiveness of a wide range of techniques, from simple linear classifiers to complex deep learning models. The uniformity of the dataset ensures that models are compared on a level playing field, and the improvements in model accuracy on MNIST have often mirrored advancements in the field of machine learning.

Convolutional Neural Networks (CNNs) for Digit Recognition

Convolutional Neural Networks (CNNs) are a class of deep learning algorithms predominantly used in processing data with a grid-like topology, such as images. A CNN's architecture is inspired by the organization of the animal visual cortex and is particularly adept at capturing spatial and temporal dependencies in an image through the application of relevant filters. The architecture of a CNN is designed to automatically and adaptively learn spatial hierarchies of features from input images.

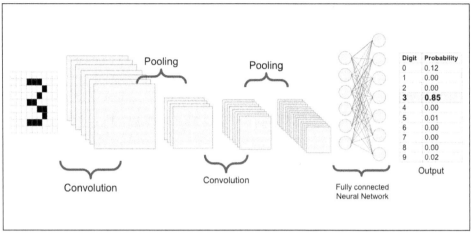

Figure 8.3: Convolutional Neural Network (CNN) Architecture

Understanding the functioning of Convolutional Neural Networks (CNNs) is key to their application in digit recognition tasks. These networks leverage a series of layers, each designed to process and transform the image data in a specific way. Below are the main types of layers in a CNN and their roles in extracting and processing features from images for digit recognition.

- **Convolutional Layers**: These are the core building blocks of a CNN. Convolutional layers apply a convolution operation to the input, passing the result to the next layer. This process involves a filter or kernel that slides over the input image, computing dot products between the entries of the filter and the input image at any position. As the filter moves across the image, a feature map is created that provides a condensed representation of the input image.

- **Pooling Layers**: Following convolutional layers, pooling layers are used to reduce the spatial dimensions (width and height) of the input volume for the next convolutional layer. The most common form of pooling is max pooling, where the maximum element is selected from the region of the feature map covered by the filter. This step reduces the computational complexity and the number of parameters.

- **Fully Connected Layers**: At the end of the network, one or more fully connected layers are used where every input is connected to every output of the previous layer. These layers are typically used to flatten the high-level features learned by convolutional layers and combine them to form the final output, such as class scores in classification tasks.

In the context of handwritten digit recognition, CNNs have proven to be exceptionally effective. They can automatically and adaptively learn spatial hierarchies of features from digit images. These features might include edges, corners, and other shape descriptors that are then used to distinguish between different digits. The ability of CNNs to capture these intricate patterns and variations in handwriting makes them well-suited for the task. Compared to traditional image processing and machine learning techniques, CNNs offer several advantages in digit recognition:

- **Feature Learning**: Unlike traditional algorithms, where features need to be hand-engineered, CNNs automatically learn the features, making them more efficient and less prone to human error.

- **Spatial Hierarchies**: CNNs can learn and understand spatial hierarchies in images, which is crucial in recognizing the structure and form of digits.

- **Robustness**: CNNs are generally more robust to variations and distortions in the input data, such as different handwriting styles and sizes.

- **Generalization**: Due to their deep architecture and ability to learn high-level features, CNNs typically generalize better to new, unseen data compared to traditional machine learning models.

Case Study: Building a Handwritten Digit Recognition Model

Embarking on the development of a handwritten digit recognition model encapsulates the essence of practical machine learning. This case study outlines a step-by-step methodology to construct a model using one of the most famous datasets in machine learning, the MNIST dataset. The process begins with establishing a development environment, followed by meticulous data preprocessing to ensure optimal training conditions. This comprehensive journey serves as a practical guide to building a machine learning model specifically designed for image recognition, covering the entire pipeline from development to evaluation.

Project Setup

To begin building a handwritten digit recognition model, you will need a Python development environment with libraries such as TensorFlow or Keras for building and training the neural network, and Matplotlib for data visualization. The MNIST dataset can be directly loaded from these libraries, simplifying the setup process.

Data Preprocessing

Data preprocessing is a series of steps that prepare the raw dataset for neural network training. It is where data becomes a format that models can ingest and learn from. Below are the detailed stages of preprocessing for the MNIST dataset.

- **Loading the Dataset**: The MNIST dataset is available in TensorFlow and Keras. You can load it using functions provided in these libraries.

- **Normalizing**: Normalize the image data to scale pixel values to a range of 0 to 1. This is done by dividing the pixel values by 255 (as pixel values range from 0 to 255).

- **Reshaping**: Since the MNIST dataset images are 28x28 pixels, reshape them into a 4D tensor (number of images, width, height, color channels). For grayscale images like MNIST, the number of color channels is 1.

- **Splitting**: Split the dataset into training and testing sets. The MNIST dataset in Keras comes pre-split, but you can further split the training set to create a validation set.

Designing the Model Architecture

The architecture of a neural network is pivotal in defining its ability to learn and make predictions. Crafting the right model involves critical decisions about its structure and components. Below are the key architectural choices to consider when building a CNN for digit recognition.

- **Layer Selection**: A typical CNN for digit recognition includes several convolutional layers, pooling layers, and fully connected layers at the end.

- **Activation Functions**: Use ReLU (Rectified Linear Unit) for the convolutional layers to keep training fast and avoid common issues like the vanishing gradient. For the final dense layer, use a softmax function to handle multi-class classification effectively.

- **Hyperparameters**: Set initial hyperparameters such as the number of filters in convolutional layers, kernel size, pool size in pooling layers, and the number of neurons in the dense layers.

Training the Model

Training the Model is the phase where the theoretical design of a neural network is put into practice. It's a process that adjusts the model's weights based on the data it processes to improve its prediction accuracy. Below are the steps involved in this crucial stage.

- **Compiling the Model**: Compile the model with an appropriate optimizer like 'adam', loss function such as 'categorical_crossentropy' for multi-class classification, and metrics like 'accuracy'.

- **Setting Learning Rate and Batch Size**: Choose a suitable learning rate (e.g., 0.001) and batch size (e.g., 32 or 64).

- **Number of Epochs**: Start with a reasonable number of epochs, such as 10, and adjust based on the performance.

- **Training**: Train the model using the fit function in Keras, passing the training data, batch size, and epochs.

Model Evaluation and Tuning

After training the model, the next essential step is to assess its effectiveness and refine its parameters for optimal performance. This phase ensures the model not only learns correctly but also generalizes well to new data. Below are the key processes involved in model evaluation and tuning.

- **Evaluating on Test Data**: Use the evaluate function to test the model's performance on the test set.

- **Tuning for Better Performance**: If the performance is not satisfactory, experiment with different architectures, hyperparameters, and training durations.

Visualizing Results

Visualizing the results of a trained model is important for understanding its learning patterns and identifying areas for improvement. It provides a visual insight into the model's performance and behavior during training. Below are the key visualization techniques used for analyzing training outcomes.

- Training Results: Plot the training and validation accuracy and loss over epochs using Matplotlib to understand how your model is learning.

- Confusion Matrix: Use a confusion matrix to see how well the model is predicting each digit.

This comprehensive guide serves as a practical framework for developing and fine-tuning neural network models, ensuring a deep understanding of each phase in the journey of machine learning model creation.

For a hands-on demonstration of the concepts discussed, refer to the accompanying coding example available at https://tinyurl.com/digitrec. This practical implementation walks you through the complete process—from loading the MNIST dataset and training a neural network, to visualizing the results using plots and confusion matrices—making it easier to connect theory with real-world application.

The Matrix and Tensor Dynamics of Image Processing

The realm of image processing, a fundamental aspect of modern technology and AI, is deeply intertwined with the concepts of matrices and tensors. In this section, we embark on an exploration of these fundamental elements, starting with an understanding of how images are represented as data structures. We delve into the core of image preprocessing techniques, unraveling the essential steps such as normalization, resizing, and augmentation that prepare images for analysis.

Understanding Image Data

Digital images are fundamentally represented as matrices of pixels, where each pixel holds a value corresponding to its intensity. In the case of grayscale images, this matrix is two-dimensional, where each element of the matrix represents a single pixel. The intensity value of each pixel in a grayscale image can vary from black, at the weakest intensity, to white, at the strongest intensity. Higher values in the matrix denote brighter intensities. For example, in an 8-bit grayscale image, the pixel values range from 0 (black) to 255 (white), which are often normalized between 0 and 1 for processing in machine learning models. This transformation is visually depicted in Figure 8.4, where an image sample is converted into raw intensity values and then structured into a tensor forma

When extending this concept to color images, the representation becomes more complex and is handled as a tensor, essentially a 3D array. Color images typically use the RGB format, meaning they are composed of three color channels: Red, Green, and Blue. Each of these channels is represented as a separate matrix, and the combination of these matrices forms the tensor representing the image. For a given pixel in a color image, there are three intensity values – one for each of the R, G, and B channels. When these channels are combined, they form the wide spectrum of colors seen in the image. This section illustrates how these layers work together, for instance, how different intensities in each channel mix to create various colors. This section illustrates how these layers work together, for instance, how different intensities in each channel mix to create various colors, as shown in Figure 8.5.

The pixel intensity values, especially in the context of color images, play a crucial role in determining the visual appearance of the image. In a standard 8-bit per channel color image, each of the R, G, and B channels can have intensity values ranging from 0 to 255. This allows for 256 different intensities per channel, combining to produce a possible palette of over 16 million colors

(256^3 combinations). The section discusses how these intensity values impact the overall color and brightness of the image. It also covers how manipulating these values can lead to various image processing techniques such as contrast enhancement, brightness adjustment, or color balancing.

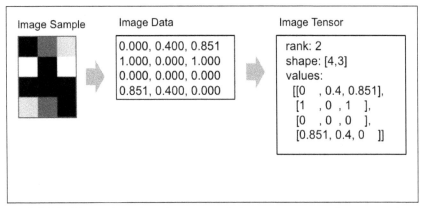

Figure 8.4: Pixel intensity values in a grayscale image represented as raw and tensor data

In the above black and white image example, we observe a 3x4 matrix representing the grayscale intensity values of the pixels. Each value in this matrix falls between 0 and 1, where 0 signifies the absence of intensity (black) and 1 corresponds to full intensity (white). The matrix format, a two-dimensional array, simplifies the grayscale image into quantifiable values that can be easily processed by computational methods. For instance, a pixel with an intensity value of 0.851 indicates a shade of gray closer to white. This grayscale matrix is then represented as a tensor of rank 2, consistent with the two dimensions it occupies—height and width.

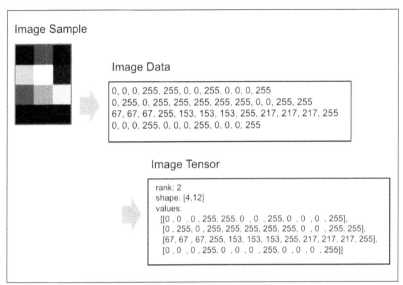

Figure 8.5: Color image representation with RGBA tensor details

The color image example in the above figure showcases a more complex structure. Here, the image is represented by a tensor of rank 2, but each element now contains a set of four values corresponding to the RGBA (Red, Green, Blue, Alpha) color channels. Unlike the grayscale image, where a single number suffices, the color image requires a combination of these four values to represent the full spectrum of colors. For example, a pixel with the values [0, 0, 255, 0] would represent a pure blue color with no transparency, as the blue channel is at full intensity while the others are at zero. The Alpha channel, often used for transparency, is also at zero in this case, which could be interpreted as fully opaque in a different context. This RGBA tensor, therefore, not only stores color information but also data about transparency, enhancing the complexity of color image processing. Each color channel, like the grayscale, ranges from 0 to 255, allowing for 256 different intensities and a combination of over 16 million possible colors. Manipulating these values affects the image's visual properties, enabling techniques such as color correction, filtering, and more advanced image processing operations.

Image Preprocessing Techniques

Image preprocessing techniques are indispensable steps in the preparation of data for machine learning and neural network training. They address the inherent variability in raw image data, transforming it into a format that is optimized for better algorithmic performance. Normalization adjusts pixel values to a common scale, enhancing model convergence and learning efficiency. Resizing ensures that all input images conform to the required dimensions of the neural network, preventing errors due to size discrepancies. Augmentation artificially expands the dataset, introducing a wealth of scenarios for the model to learn from, thus preventing overfitting and promoting robustness. Collectively, these techniques are pivotal for fine-tuning the dataset, enabling the development of machine learning models that are capable of extracting meaningful patterns and achieving high accuracy in various image recognition tasks.

Normalization: Normalization is a key preprocessing step in the preparation of image data for use in neural network training. This process involves scaling the pixel values of an image to a smaller, standardized range, typically between 0 and 1. In an image, pixel values can range up to 255 (in the case of 8-bit images), and directly using these values can lead to issues in training neural networks due to the large variance in input data.

The reason normalization is essential is that neural networks tend to learn and converge faster when the input data resides within a smaller range. This is partly due to the way weights are updated in the network during the backpropagation process. When input data vary widely, the gradient updates can also vary significantly, leading to unstable training and making it difficult for the network to converge. By scaling down the input data, normalization helps in achieving a more stable and faster convergence.

In practice, normalization is done by dividing the pixel values of an image by 255 (the maximum pixel value), which scales all the values down to a range between 0 and 1. This scaling does not change the content or the structure of the image but makes the data more suitable for processing by the neural network.

Resizing: Resizing images to a consistent size is another fundamental preprocessing step in preparing data for neural networks. Neural networks require a fixed size of the input layer, and hence, all input images must have the same dimensions.

The challenge arises from the fact that real-world image datasets often contain images of varying sizes and aspect ratios. Feeding images of different sizes into a neural network is not feasible as it can lead to errors or skewed results. Therefore, resizing is used to standardize the dimensions of all images in a dataset.

This process involves changing the width and height of an image to match the required input dimensions of the neural network while trying to preserve the aspect ratio to avoid distortion. Techniques like cropping, padding, or using aspect ratio preserving scaling are common. It's important to consider the effect of resizing on the image content, as drastic resizing might lead to loss of crucial details or introduce unwanted distortions.

Augmentation: Image augmentation is a technique used to expand the diversity of a dataset by applying various transformations to the images. This process not only increases the quantity of the data but also introduces a variety of scenarios under which the model should perform accurately. Common augmentation techniques include:

- **Rotation**: Rotating the image by a certain angle to simulate the effect of tilt or uneven camera angles.

- **Translation**: Shifting the image horizontally or vertically, which helps the model learn to recognize objects no matter where they appear in the image.

- **Scaling**: Enlarging or shrinking the image. This simulates the effect of objects being closer or farther away from the camera.

- **Flipping**: Mirroring the image either horizontally or vertically. This is particularly useful in cases where the orientation is not fixed.

- **Adding Noise:** Introducing random pixel-level noise can make the model more robust to variations in image quality.

Augmentation helps in building a more robust model by ensuring it does not learn to overfit to the specificities of the training data and can generalize well to new, unseen data that may vary in many ways from the training set. This is particularly important in real-world applications where the conditions under which images are captured can vary significantly.

Feature Extraction in Images

Convolutional Neural Networks (CNNs) play an important role in the automatic and efficient extraction of features from images. The architecture of a CNN is uniquely suited for this task due to its use of convolutional layers that apply filters to the input images. These filters are essentially small matrices that move across the image and perform dot products with the pixel values they cover. This operation allows the network to capture various aspects of the image, such as edges, textures, or patterns.

The power of CNNs in feature extraction lies in their ability to learn the most relevant filters for the task during the training process. Initially, these filters are set randomly, but through the process of backpropagation and gradient descent, the network adjusts these filters to capture features that are most useful for the classification or recognition task at hand. This automatic feature extraction is a significant departure from traditional methods, where features had to be hand-engineered and carefully selected.

In a CNN, each layer is responsible for extracting different levels of features. The early layers typically capture basic features such as edges, lines, and simple textures. These are the fundamental building blocks of more complex patterns. As the image data progresses through the network, each subsequent layer combines and transforms these basic features to capture more complex and abstract representations of the image.

For instance, in a facial recognition task, the initial layers might detect edges and contours, while the middle layers might identify parts of a face like eyes, noses, or mouths. In the deeper layers, these features are combined to form a high-level representation of the face, which the network can then use to distinguish between different individuals.

Structuring Data for Image Processing and the role of Convolution Kernels

In image processing, how data is structured and manipulated plays a central role in achieving efficient and accurate results. This section delves into the crucial aspects of organizing and structuring data for optimal processing efficiency. We begin by exploring the best practices in data structuring, which is fundamental for handling and processing images effectively. Then, we shift our focus to the heart of image processing techniques - convolution kernels. Here, we explain their critical function, how they work, and their significant role in feature detection and image processing. Finally, we bridge theory with practice by providing insights into the practical application of designing and tuning convolution kernels. This includes strategies for customizing and optimizing these kernels to enhance the performance of image processing tasks, illustrating a blend of theoretical knowledge and practical skills essential in this field.

Data Structuring for Efficient Processing

Data structuring for efficient processing is a fundamental concept in machine learning that involves organizing and formatting data in a way that machines can understand and process effectively. As we begin exploring key aspects like data storage, batch processing, pipeline optimization, and memory management, it's important to understand that the strategies we adopt in these areas can significantly impact the performance and scalability of machine learning models. Properly structured data ensures not only efficiency in processing but also accuracy and robustness in the resulting analytical outcomes. This underlying structure forms the backbone of our ability to extract meaningful insights from vast amounts of visual data.

Data Storage and Organization

The way image data is stored and organized plays a critical role in the efficiency of image processing and machine learning tasks. Different file formats for storing image data, such as JPEG, PNG, and TIFF, have distinct characteristics that impact both the quality of the image data and the speed of processing.

- **JPEG**: This is a commonly used format for storing images, especially for photographs. JPEG uses lossy compression, reducing file size significantly but at the cost of some loss of image quality. This format is suitable for real-world images where slight quality loss is acceptable.

- **PNG**: PNG format is used for images where quality and details are crucial. It uses lossless compression, meaning no image data is lost during saving. PNG is ideal for tasks requiring high precision in image details, such as medical imaging or technical illustrations.

- **TIFF**: TIFF is often used in professional photography and publishing due to its ability to store image data in a lossless format with high depth (like 16-bit or 32-bit images). However, TIFF files are generally larger, impacting the speed of data processing.

The choice of file format can significantly impact the efficiency of image processing workflows, with trade-offs between file size, quality, and processing speed.

Batch Processing

Batch processing is a vital concept in neural network training, where data is divided into smaller, manageable groups or 'batches' for processing. This approach has several advantages:

- Efficient Use of Computational Resources: By processing data in batches, neural networks can effectively utilize memory and computational resources, such as GPU acceleration. It allows for parallel processing of data, leading to faster training times.

- Stability in Learning: Batching helps in stabilizing the learning process. It averages out the noise in the gradient updates, leading to smoother convergence during training.

- Flexibility in Memory Usage: Batch processing provides flexibility in managing memory usage, as the batch size can be adjusted based on the available system memory.

Data Pipeline Optimization

Efficient data pipeline design is essential for high-performance processing, especially when handling large datasets. A well-optimized pipeline reduces bottlenecks, improves throughput, and ensures smoother data flow throughout the training process. Below are key strategies commonly used to enhance pipeline performance:

- Data Generators: For very large datasets that cannot fit into memory, data generators can be used to load and process data on-the-fly, effectively bypassing memory limitations.

- Efficient Loading and Preprocessing: Techniques like multi-threaded data loading and preprocessing can significantly reduce the time spent in these stages. This includes optimizing image reading, resizing, and normalization processes.

- Parallel Processing: Leveraging parallel processing capabilities of modern hardware can drastically improve the efficiency of the data pipeline. This involves distributing data processing tasks across multiple cores or GPUs.

Memory Management

Effective memory management is key in handling large datasets:

- In-Memory vs. On-Disk Storage: Choosing whether to store data in memory or on disk is an important decision that impacts performance and scalability. In-memory processing is faster but limited by RAM size, while on-disk processing allows handling larger datasets at the cost of speed.

- Reducing Memory Footprint: Techniques such as image compression (without significant loss of quality) and down-sampling (reducing the resolution of images) can help in reducing the memory footprint of the dataset.

Convolution Kernels

Convolution kernels, also known as filters, are fundamental to the process of image processing, particularly in the context of Convolutional Neural Networks (CNNs). These kernels are essentially small matrices or grids of numbers that are used to transform an image into a feature map through the process of convolution.

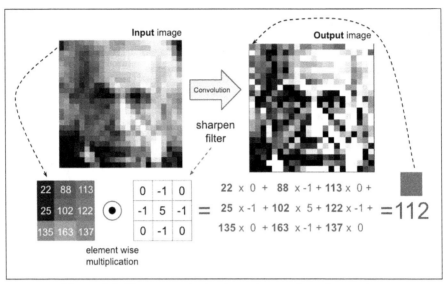

Figure 8.6: How convolution kernels transform image data

The kernel slides over the input image, and at each position, a mathematical operation is performed. This operation involves element-wise multiplication of the kernel values with the pixel values of the image it covers, followed by summing up these products. The result is a single pixel in the feature map, and this process is repeated across the entire image. The primary purpose of using convolution kernels is to extract features from images. Depending on the values in the kernel, different features of the image can be highlighted. For instance, certain kernels can accentuate edges, while others may blur out details. The interaction between convolution kernels and images is grounded in mathematical operations that transform the image in various ways.

The "Sharpen" filter illustrated in the above image is a type of convolution kernel used to enhance the edges and details of an image. The filter is represented by a 3x3 matrix with a specific pattern of numbers: a central value of 5 surrounded by -1s. This configuration is particularly effective at highlighting transitions in intensity, which correspond to edges and fine details. When the "Sharpen" filter is applied to an image, it accentuates the contrast at the edges. This is achieved by the element-wise multiplication of the filter with the pixel values of the image. For instance, in the illustrated example, a portion of the image where the filter is applied has pixel values of 22, 88, 113, and so on. Each of these values is multiplied by the corresponding value in the filter matrix. The central pixel, multiplied by 5, gains more weight, while the surrounding pixels, multiplied by -1, are subtracted, emphasizing the difference between the central pixel and its neighbors. The sum of these products yields a new value that replaces the central pixel in the feature map. In the example, the sum is 112, which will be the new value of the pixel in the output image at that location. By repeating this operation across the entire image, the "Sharpen" filter enhances the overall sharpness and clarity, making it a commonly used technique in image processing to improve visual appeal and aid in feature detection for further analysis.

Below is the list of some of the most common filters used in image processing, each with a brief description of their function:

- **Sharpen**: Intensifies edges and fine details in the image by increasing the contrast between neighboring pixels.

- **Blur**: Smoothens the image by averaging the pixels' values, reducing detail and noise.

- **Emboss**: Gives the image a three-dimensional effect by highlighting edges from a particular direction, as if the image is raised above the background.

- **Outline**: Detects and highlights the outlines of objects within the image by emphasizing the boundaries.

- **Identity**: Leaves the image unchanged; this filter is effectively a no-operation and is used to maintain the original image.

- **Top Sobel**: Emphasizes horizontal edges in the upper part of the image, typically used for edge detection in the vertical direction.

- **Bottom Sobel**: Similar to the top Sobel filter but focuses on horizontal edges in the lower part of the image.

- **Left Sobel**: Highlights vertical edges on the left side of the image, used for edge detection in the horizontal direction.

- **Right Sobel**: This filter is the counterpart to the left Sobel, accentuating vertical edges on the right side of the image.

Each of these filters acts as a convolution kernel that, when applied to an image, transforms the pixel values through the convolution operation to produce the desired effect, thus playing a key role in feature extraction and image enhancement. The mathematical process behind these transformations involves linear operations characterized by the convolutional kernel matrix. This process fundamentally alters the pixel values of the image, resulting in different visual representations based on the kernel used.

Pooling Layers

Pooling layers are another component of CNNs, usually placed after convolutional layers. Their primary function is to reduce the spatial dimensions (width and height) of the feature maps obtained from the convolutional layers. This reduction not only decreases the computational load and the number of parameters in the network but also helps in making the network more robust to slight variations and distortions in the input image.

The most common type of pooling is max pooling, where the maximum value from a group of pixels in the feature map is retained. This process effectively summarizes the most prominent features in a particular region of the feature map while discarding less significant details.

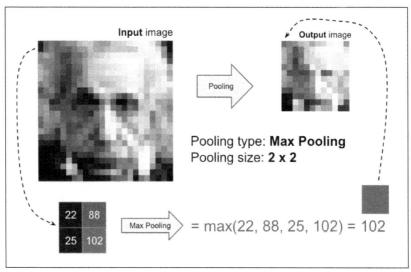

Figure 8.7: Max pooling operation for feature map down-sampling

The "Max Pooling" operation is exemplified in the above image, demonstrating a common technique within CNNs to down-sample the feature map, thus reducing its dimensions. In this specific example, a 2x2 max pooling

142

filter is applied to the input image. This filter moves over the feature map and, at each position, selects the maximum pixel value from the 2x2 square of pixels it covers. For instance, the highlighted 2x2 region in the input image contains the pixel values 22, 88, 25, and 102. The max pooling operation takes these values and computes the maximum; in this case, 102 is the largest value. This value is then used as a single pixel in the new, down-sampled output feature map. By applying this operation across the entire input feature map, max pooling effectively reduces the spatial dimensions by a factor determined by the size of the pooling filter, which is 2x2 in this example. Consequently, the output image after max pooling shows a reduced number of pixels, summarizing the most critical features while discarding the less significant details. This process contributes to the reduction of computational requirements and improves the network's ability to generalize by focusing on the most salient features.

Designing and Tuning Convolution Kernels

In the quest to harness the full potential of Convolutional Neural Networks (CNNs), the practical application of designing and tuning convolution kernels stands as a cornerstone technique. These kernels, integral to feature extraction and image analysis, require careful crafting and continual refinement to meet the specific needs of varied image processing tasks. Tailoring the architecture of these kernels – their size, shape, and pattern of values – is both an art and a science, demanding a deep understanding of the underlying mathematics and a willingness to engage in iterative experimentation. The upcoming sections will walk you through this process in detail—starting with the fundamentals of designing custom kernels, followed by practical strategies for tuning them, and concluding with advanced techniques like automated kernel optimization. Together, these topics build a comprehensive understanding of how to tailor convolution kernels for specific tasks in deep learning.

Designing Custom Kernels

Custom convolution kernels are designed to perform specific image processing tasks, and their effectiveness depends on various factors like size, shape, and the underlying mathematics.

- **Kernel Size and Shape**: The size of the kernel (e.g., 3x3, 5x5) determines the area of the input image that the kernel covers at any given time. Smaller kernels are more suited for detecting fine details, while larger kernels are better for capturing broader features. The shape of the kernel can be adjusted to target specific orientations or patterns within the image.

- **Detecting Specific Features**: The arrangement of values within a kernel dictates the type of feature it can detect. For example, a kernel with a horizontal line of high values will be effective in highlighting horizontal edges. Designing these kernels requires an understanding of how different patterns in the kernel values interact with the image.

- **Experimentation and Testing**: Designing effective custom kernels often involves a process of experimentation and testing. Adjusting the values and observing the resulting output helps in refining the kernel for the desired task.

Tuning and Optimization

Optimizing convolution kernels in a neural network is a critical step to enhance performance and accuracy.

- **Selecting Kernel Numbers and Sizes**: The number of kernels and their sizes in each layer of a CNN should be chosen based on the complexity of the features to be detected. More complex images may require a higher number of kernels to capture the intricacies.

- **Learning Rates**: Setting an appropriate learning rate is important. A learning rate that's too high may cause the network to miss the optimal solution, while a rate that's too low may lead to excessively slow convergence.

- **Kernel Initialization**: Proper initialization of kernel weights can significantly impact the training process. Techniques like Xavier or He initialization can be used depending on the activation function in the network.

- **Avoiding Overfitting**: Techniques such as dropout, regularization, or using a proper validation set can help in preventing the network from overfitting, ensuring that the kernels generalize well to new data.

Summary

This chapter explores into the rapidly evolving field of artificial intelligence, with a particular focus on the use of deep learning for visual recognition tasks. This chapter comprehensively explores the fundamentals of image processing and advanced techniques in pattern recognition, highlighting the pivotal role of convolutional neural networks (CNNs) in revolutionizing the interpretation and understanding of visual data. It begins with an insightful discussion of the application of deep learning to handwritten digit identification, a benchmark problem in neural networks for visual recognition. The chapter then discusses in detail the nuances of matrix and tensor dynamics that are essential for processing and understanding image data, and delves into data structuring for image processing, with a special emphasis on the role of convolutional kernels in feature extraction and image interpretation.

Chapter 9: Audio Recognition and Processing in AI

This chapter introduces the domain of audio recognition within the context of artificial intelligence. It provides an overview of the key concepts and challenges involved in processing audio data, a field that merges technological development with human-like auditory interpretation. It explores how AI systems are trained to interpret and understand audio signals, from the simplest tones to the complexity of human speech and natural sounds. The focus is not only on the mechanisms by which AI recognizes these sounds but also on the processing techniques involved, highlighting the significant role of algorithms like the Fast Fourier Transform (FFT) in breaking down and analyzing sound spectra. This comprehensive exploration provides insights into how these technologies are transforming the way machines interact with the auditory world, making it an invaluable resource for anyone interested in the convergence of AI and audio processing.

Introduction to Audio Recognition in AI

Audio recognition technology has come a long way since its inception. Initially, the focus was on simple tone recognition, used in early telephone systems to recognize dial tones. This evolved into voice command recognition in the late 20th century, where systems could understand basic spoken commands but struggled with complexity and accents. The breakthrough came with the introduction of machine learning and neural networks, which significantly improved the accuracy and adaptability of audio recognition systems. In the past decade, deep learning has taken this a step further, allowing for real-time, natural language processing and even emotional tone analysis. Today, audio recognition is not only about understanding speech but also identifying various sounds and their contexts, making it an ever-evolving field in AI.

The applications of audio recognition technology span numerous domains. In security, voice recognition systems are used for authentication and surveillance. In healthcare, audio analysis assists in diagnosing conditions like sleep apnea or monitoring mental health through voice changes. Virtual assistants like Siri and Alexa rely heavily on audio recognition to interpret and respond to user commands. In entertainment, this technology is used in everything from interactive games to music composition and analysis. The versatility of audio recognition makes it a valuable tool across different sectors, improving user experience, enhancing security measures, and even aiding in medical diagnostics.

At the heart of audio recognition are a few key principles. Firstly, understanding sound waves and their characteristics such as frequency, amplitude, and phase is crucial. This knowledge helps in digitally representing audio signals for processing. Digital Signal Processing (DSP) then comes into play, which involves sampling and quantization to convert these sounds into a format that can be analyzed by algorithms. Features like Mel-frequency cepstral coefficients (MFCCs) are often extracted from these signals for pattern recognition. Machine learning models, particularly neural networks, are trained to recognize these patterns and interpret them accordingly. This combination of sound wave analysis, DSP, and machine learning forms the cornerstone of modern audio recognition systems.

The Role of FFT in Audio Recognition and Sound Spectrum Analysis

The Fast Fourier Transform (FFT) is a fundamental algorithm in the field of digital signal processing, playing a crucial role in audio recognition. It is a method for efficiently computing the Discrete Fourier Transform (DFT), which converts a signal from its original time domain into the frequency domain. The time domain shows how a signal changes over time, while the frequency domain represents the signal in terms of its frequency content. The FFT algorithm decomposes a time-based signal into its constituent frequencies, revealing the amplitude and phase of each frequency component. This transformation is key in analyzing audio signals, as it allows for the identification and isolation of different sound elements based on their frequency characteristics.

In audio processing, FFT is used to analyze the frequency content of audio signals. For voice recognition, FFT helps in distinguishing between different phonemes (distinct units of sound) by breaking down the voice signal into its frequency components. This frequency-based analysis is critical in identifying and differentiating various sounds and speech elements. In music analysis, FFT is used to identify musical notes, chords, and rhythms by analyzing the frequency spectrum of a musical piece. It enables the detection of different instruments in a song and can even be used for audio effects like equalization, where certain frequency bands are amplified or attenuated.

FFT's role in AI extends to various practical applications:

- **Speech Recognition**: AI systems like virtual assistants use FFT to analyze speech patterns. By breaking down speech into frequency components, these systems can more accurately recognize words and phrases, even in noisy environments.

- **Sound Classification**: In AI-driven sound classification, FFT is used to analyze environmental sounds or machinery noises for monitoring and diagnostic purposes. For instance, identifying the sound of a failing machine part in a factory setting for predictive maintenance.

- **Noise Reduction**: In applications like call centers or voice-activated systems, FFT is instrumental in noise reduction algorithms. By analyzing the frequency spectrum of the audio, AI systems can filter out background noise, enhancing the clarity of the spoken words.

- **Audio Fingerprinting**: FFT is used in creating unique fingerprints of audio tracks, which AI systems can then use to identify songs or detect copyright infringements.

Understanding FFT (Fast Fourier Transform) in Audio Signals

Audio signals are inherently complex, comprising a myriad of frequencies. Grasping their composition is essential for pattern recognition within sounds. The FFT is a mathematical apparatus that decomposes an audio signal into its elemental frequencies, thus presenting it in a format that is more suitable for interpretation by neural networks. This procedure parallels the transformation of images into numerical arrays for image recognition, where FFT converts audio signals into a frequency spectrum, providing valuable input for deep learning models. Such a transformation empowers neural networks to discern and differentiate between diverse sound forms, including music, speech, or environmental noise.

Transforming Audio into Digital Signal

The first step in audio processing is converting the analog audio signal into a digital signal. This involves sampling the audio wave at regular intervals. The sampling rate, usually measured in Hz (samples per second), determines the resolution of the digital audio. A standard CD-quality audio, for example, has a sampling rate of 44.1 kHz.

The Spectrogram

Once the audio signal is digitized, we can represent it as a spectrogram. A spectrogram is a visual representation of the spectrum of frequencies in a sound signal as they vary with time. In simpler terms, it's a graph that shows how different frequencies present in the audio signal fluctuate over time. The x-axis represents time, the y-axis represents frequency, and the intensity of colors in the graph indicates the amplitude (or loudness) of various frequencies at different times.

FFT and Its Mathematical Foundation

The Fast Fourier Transform (FFT) is used to convert the time-domain audio signal into a frequency-domain representation. The mathematical basis of FFT lies in the Fourier Transform, which decomposes a function of time (a signal) into its constituent frequencies. The Fourier Transform of a continuous time-domain signal

$$X(f) = \int_{-\infty}^{\infty} x(t)e^{-j2\pi ft}dt$$

Where:

- X(f) is the frequency domain representation,

- f is the frequency,

- t is time, and

- $e^{-j2\pi ft}$ is a complex exponential function.

The FFT algorithm efficiently computes this transformation for discrete signals, making it feasible to process even in real-time applications. The discrete Fourier Transform (DFT) for a discrete time-domain signal x[n] is given by:

$$X[k] = \sum_{n=0}^{N-1} x[n]e^{-j2\pi kn/N}$$

Where:

- X[k] is the discrete frequency domain representation,

- N is the total number of samples,

- k represents the index of the frequency bin, and

- n represents the time index.

- $e^{-j2\pi kn/N}$ is the basis function for the FFT, a complex exponential function where j is the imaginary unit.

This equation translates a sequence of N complex numbers x[n] from the time domain into N complex numbers X[k] in the frequency domain. The FFT is an algorithmic strategy to calculate the same results as the DFT with significantly less computational effort. While the DFT requires $O(N^2)$ operations to compute, the FFT reduces this complexity to O(NlogN) by cleverly factoring and reusing results of smaller DFTs. This efficiency gain is achieved by breaking down the DFT into smaller DFTs recursively, exploiting the periodic and symmetrical properties of the complex exponential functions.

Example of Fast Fourier Transform (FFT)

This section introduces an example to explain the Fast Fourier Transform (FFT). It sets the stage for a demonstration using a simple signal composed of three distinct frequencies. This example is foundational for understanding how FFT analyzes and breaks down complex signals into their constituent frequencies.

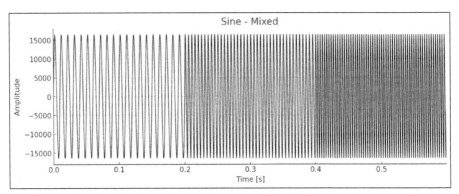

Figure 9.1: Audio signal with three combined frequencies over time.

The above image, Figure 9.1, depicts a signal comprising three frequencies: 100 Hz, 200 Hz, and 300 Hz, each spanning approximately 0.2 seconds. On the x-axis, we have time, reflecting the duration over which the signal extends, and on the y-axis, amplitude is displayed, indicating the strength or loudness of the signal at any given point in time. This visual representation helps in understanding how these three different frequencies are combined over time to form a composite audio signal

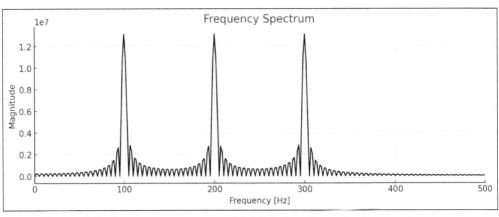

Figure 9.2: Frequency spectrum highlighting three distinct peaks

Here in the above image, the frequency spectrum plot clearly showcases the three distinct frequencies present in the signal. The x-axis represents the frequency in Hertz (Hz), showing the range of frequencies contained in the signal, while the y-axis represents the magnitude, indicating how prominent each frequency is within the signal. The presence of peaks at 100 Hz, 200 Hz, and 300 Hz confirms the composition of the signal as described earlier.

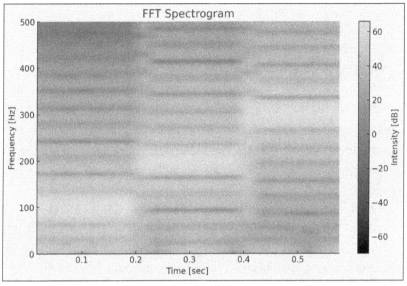

Figure 9.3: FFT spectrogram showing how frequencies change over time

The above image, Figure 9.3, is the FFT spectrogram of the signal containing the three frequencies. The x-axis of the spectrogram represents time, similar to the second image, while the y-axis now represents frequency. The color intensity in the spectrogram indicates the amplitude or strength of a particular frequency at a given time. This visual tool effectively illustrates how the frequencies of the signal vary over time, providing a comprehensive view of both the temporal and frequency aspects of the signal. This spectral representation, achieved through the application of the Fast Fourier Transform (FFT), provides the following detailed analysis of the frequency components within the signal. The frame size or window size used in the FFT spectrogram computation is 256 samples.

- **Peaks at 100 Hz, 200 Hz, and 300 Hz**: These peaks are indicative of the presence of these specific frequencies within the signal. Each peak corresponds to a frequency component, with its height representing the magnitude or strength of that frequency at a particular point in time.

- **Significance of Peaks**: The existence of these peaks in the spectrogram is a direct confirmation of the signal's composition. In the context of audio processing, this kind of analysis is crucial for identifying different tones, notes, or sound characteristics. It's particularly useful in scenarios like music production, audio engineering, and signal processing research.

- **Temporal Resolution**: Unlike the previous frequency spectrum plot which showed the aggregate presence of frequencies over the entire signal duration, the spectrogram adds another layer of insight by showing how these frequencies vary over time. This temporal resolution allows for a more nuanced understanding of the signal's dynamics.

- **Color Coding**: The intensity of colors in the spectrogram typically represents the amplitude of frequencies at various points in time. Brighter or more intense colors at certain frequencies and times indicate higher amplitudes of those frequencies.

Next is a much simpler (toy) example of FFT computation. Here we have a Sine wave signal expressed in a table and a graph form. The frequency of this signal is 1 Hz. The sampling period, the time interval between the signal measurements, is 0.083 seconds. In terms of sampling frequency, it is 1/0.083 or 12 Hz.

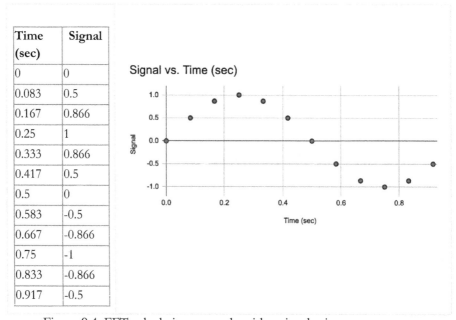

Time (sec)	Signal
0	0
0.083	0.5
0.167	0.866
0.25	1
0.333	0.866
0.417	0.5
0.5	0
0.583	-0.5
0.667	-0.866
0.75	-1
0.833	-0.866
0.917	-0.5

Figure 9.4: FFT calculation example with a simple sine wave

Now to calculate the FFT, we use the below formula. The X[k] value gives us the FFT magnitude for a discrete frequency (bucket) k.

$$X[k] = \sum_{n=0}^{N-1} x[n] e^{-j2\pi kn/N}$$

Where:

- X[k] is the discrete frequency domain representation,

- N is the total number of samples,

- k represents the index of the frequency bin, and

- n represents the time index.

- $e^{-j2\pi kn/N}$ is the basis function for the FFT, a complex exponential function where j is the imaginary unit.

To make things easy to understand let's use 12 frequency bins (0 through 11) each separated by 1 Hz so k = 0, 1, 2, ... 12. Also let's resolve the complex exponential function in the above equation into its real and imaginary parts and then compute the magnitude using the below formulas.

$$\text{Re}\{X[k]\} = \sum_{n=0}^{N-1} x[n] \cdot \cos(2\pi kn/N)$$

$$\text{Im}\{X[k]\} = - \sum_{n=0}^{N-1} x[n] \cdot \sin(2\pi kn/N)$$

$$FFT\ Magnitude = |X[k]| = \sqrt{(\text{Re}\{X[k]\})^2 + (\text{Im}\{X[k]\})^2}$$

Below is a sample calculation for k = 1;

Re{X[1]} = 0.00 + 0.43 + 0.43 + 0.00 - 0.43 - 0.43 + 0.00 + 0.43 + 0.43 + 0.00 - 0.43 - 0.43 = **0.0**

Im{X[1]} − 0.00 - 0.25 - 0.75 - 1.00 - 0.75 - 0.25 + 0.00 - 0.25 - 0.75 - 1.00 - 0.75 - 0.25 = **-6.0**

$$FFT\ Magnitude = \sqrt{(0.0)^2 + (-0.6)^2} = 0.6$$

Calculating the FFT Magnitude for all frequency bins (k = 0 through 11), the results can be shown as below table and the bar chart. Please notice the presence of the 1 Hz frequency in the FFT table and the chart.

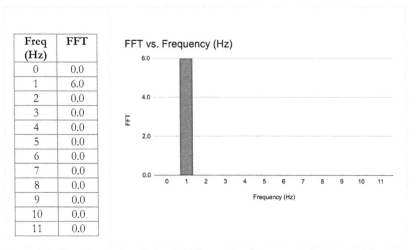

Freq (Hz)	FFT
0	0.0
1	6.0
2	0.0
3	0.0
4	0.0
5	0.0
6	0.0
7	0.0
8	0.0
9	0.0
10	0.0
11	0.0

Figure 9.5: Bar chart visualizing FFT magnitudes across frequency bins

Audio Recognition with Speech Commands: A Simple Example

Embarking on the journey of Audio Recognition with Speech Commands, this comprehensive guide serves as your beacon through the intricate process of transforming spoken language into a format that machine learning algorithms can understand and process. From setting up your programming environment with TensorFlow to the deployment of the Mini Speech Commands dataset, each step is designed to lead you to the heart of audio recognition: a finely tuned model capable of deciphering the subtle nuances of human speech.

The Mini Speech Commands Dataset

The Mini Speech Commands dataset is a compact version of the original Speech Commands dataset developed by Google. It was designed to support simple voice recognition tasks by providing a smaller yet representative sample of audio data. This curated dataset includes short recordings of individual spoken words, making it well-suited for training lightweight machine learning models. Its diverse and balanced composition helps reduce potential biases in training, while the standardized format—each clip representing a single word—offers clarity and ease of use for developing and testing speech recognition systems..

This dataset embodies a rich variety of phonetic contexts by including multiple utterances of words spoken by different individuals. Such variance is essential for generalization, allowing models trained on this dataset to recognize commands across different speakers, accents, and intonations.

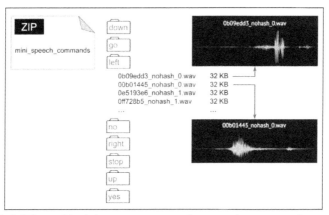

Figure 9.6: Hierarchical dataset structure for speech command recognition

The structure of the dataset facilitates machine learning tasks by organizing files into directories corresponding to each word label. This hierarchical format simplifies access and manipulation of data during training, validation, and testing phases.

With thousands of audio clips, each labeled with a keyword such as "yes," "no," "stop," or "go," the dataset is an ideal starting point for building speech recognition systems. It is particularly valuable for training models to understand and respond to voice commands, a feature increasingly in demand across a variety of technology domains.

Spectrogram Synthesis - Deciphering Audio Signatures

As introduced earlier, converting raw audio waveforms into spectrograms is a transformative step that enables Convolutional Neural Networks (CNNs) to effectively process sound. This section focuses on spectrogram synthesis—a complex yet powerful technique that translates the temporal fluctuations of audio signals into structured representations of frequency and time. These representations serve as visual patterns that CNNs can analyze and interpret with precision.

Spectrograms offer a vivid depiction of sound, revealing the intensity of various frequencies over time. Each pixel in this two-dimensional graph encodes the amplitude of a particular frequency at a given moment, painting a comprehensive portrait of the sound's spectral evolution. This visual representation is crucial for CNNs to discern patterns within the audio data.

At the heart of spectrogram synthesis lies the Short-Time Fourier Transform (STFT), a mathematical operation that dissects the audio waveform into segments and applies the Fourier Transform to each, extracting the frequency content

The process begins with slicing the audio waveform into overlapping frames, each multiplied by a windowing function to minimize edge artifacts. The Fourier Transform is then applied to each frame, transforming the time-domain data into the frequency domain. The result is a sequence of frequency spectra, which, when combined, form the complete spectrogram. Below are the FFT Spectrograms of 2 speech samples of the word "left".

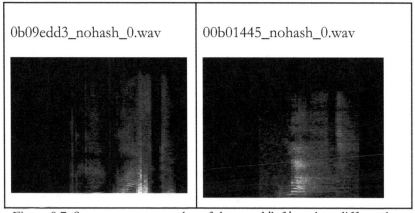

Figure 9.7: Spectrogram examples of the word 'left' spoken differently

Once the spectrograms are computed, they are prepared for ingestion by the CNN. This involves normalizing the spectrogram intensities, ensuring they fall within a range conducive to neural network training, and potentially resizing the spectrogram images to meet the input dimensions required by the CNN architecture.

CNN Construction - Architecting the Audio Decoder

In the world of audio recognition, the construction of a Convolutional Neural Network (CNN) is akin to crafting a sophisticated decoder. This section ventures into the assembly of a CNN using TensorFlow's Keras API, illustrating how each meticulously designed layer contributes to deciphering the complex patterns within audio spectrograms.

Layer-by-Layer Synthesis

The CNN's architecture is composed of several key layers, each with a distinct function:

- Resizing Layer: Adapts the input spectrograms to a uniform size, ensuring compatibility with the network's architecture.

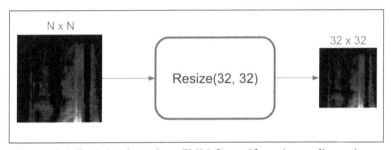

Figure 9.8: Resizing layer in a CNN for uniform input dimensions

- Normalization Layer: Standardizes the input data by adjusting its range, enhancing the network's learning efficiency. This layer normalizes each pixel in the spectrogram based on its mean and standard deviation.

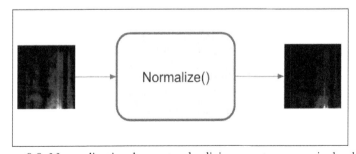

Figure 9.9: Normalization layer standardizing spectrogram pixel values

- Convolutional Layers: The cornerstone of the CNN, these layers apply various filters to the input, extracting salient features. Each convolutional layer learns to recognize different patterns, from basic edges to more complex textures and shapes.

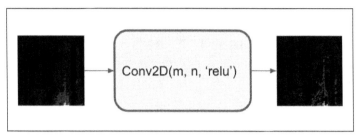

Figure 9.10: Convolutional layers extracting audio features from spectrograms

- Activation Function (ReLU): Integrated within convolutional layers, the Rectified Linear Unit (ReLU) activation function introduces non-linearity, allowing the network to learn complex patterns.

- Pooling Layers: Follow the convolutional layers, reducing the spatial dimensions of the feature maps. This downsampling process not only reduces computational load but also helps in achieving translational invariance.

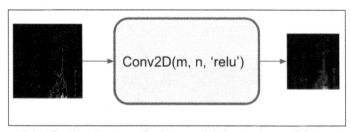

Figure 9.11: Pooling layers reducing spatial dimensions of feature maps

- Dropout Layers: These layers randomly deactivate a subset of neurons, preventing overfitting and encouraging distributed learning.

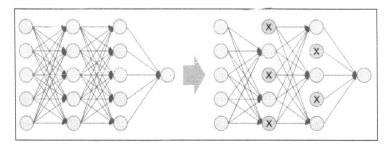

Figure 9.12: Dropout layer preventing overfitting by deactivating neurons

- Flatten Layer: Converts the 2D feature maps into a 1D vector, preparing the data for the final fully connected layers.

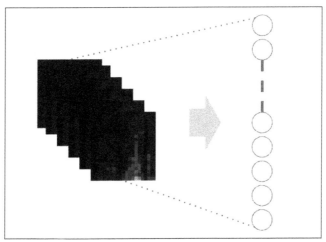

Figure 9.13: Flatten layer converting 2D feature maps into a 1D vector

- Dense Layers: Fully connected layers that synthesize the learned features into high-level representations, culminating in the output layer that classifies the audio inputs into distinct categories.

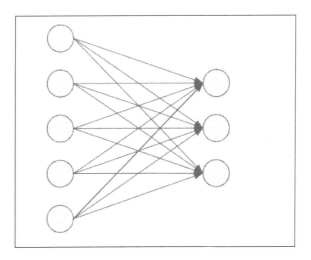

Figure 9.14: Dense layers synthesizing features into class probabilities

Each layer in the CNN operates harmoniously, transforming raw spectrogram inputs into a refined understanding of audio content. The layer-by-layer construction ensures that complex features are extracted and interpreted effectively, enabling the CNN to perform nuanced audio recognition tasks.

The below image combines all the stages described above to form a complete visual flowchart of the convolutional neural network (CNN) designed for audio recognition tasks. This diagrammatic representation encapsulates the sequential processing steps, starting from the raw input to the final classification output. The initial stages, including the resize and normalization layers, prepare the audio spectrogram for feature detection. This is followed by a series of convolutional layers that act as feature extractors, capturing the essence of the audio signal's texture and patterns through filter applications.

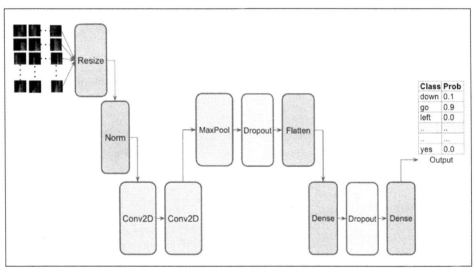

Figure 9.15: Complete CNN architecture for audio recognition tasks

As the signal progresses through the network, the pooling layers reduce dimensionality, enhancing computational efficiency and feature robustness. Dropout layers interspersed within the network architecture mitigate the risk of overfitting by randomly omitting neuron connections during training. This randomness encourages the model to learn more general features that are not dependent on the specific training data. The transition from multi-dimensional feature maps to a flat, one-dimensional array is accomplished through the flattening process, which is essential for connecting convolutional layers to dense layers.

The culmination of the CNN's processing is seen in the dense layers, where all learned representations are integrated and interpreted. These fully connected layers distill the myriad of features into a form suitable for classification, ultimately leading to the output layer. Here, each category is assigned a probability score, reflecting the confidence of the model in its predictions. The category with the highest probability score is chosen as the final output, completing the network's task of classifying the audio input into a defined category.

Model Compilation - Fine-tuning the Acoustic Decoder

Compiling the CNN is a critical step in fine-tuning the neural network for the task of audio recognition. This stage involves selecting the right optimizer and loss function to guide the model's learning process.

Choosing the Optimizer

The Adam optimizer is often the optimizer of choice due to its effectiveness and efficiency. It combines the benefits of two other extensions of stochastic gradient descent: Adaptive Gradient Algorithm (AdaGrad) and Root Mean Square Propagation (RMSProp). Adam adjusts the learning rate throughout training, which helps navigate the complex landscapes of high-dimensional data more effectively.

Selecting the Loss Function

For multi-class classification tasks, the sparse categorical cross-entropy loss function is typically employed. This function measures the disparity between the actual label and the predicted probability distribution across various classes. It is particularly suited for scenarios where the classes are mutually exclusive, which is often the case in audio recognition tasks.

The Technical Essence

The chapter delves into the nuances of these choices, explaining how the Adam optimizer dynamically updates learning rates for different parameters, thereby enhancing the model's ability to converge to an optimal solution. It also elaborates on the mathematical underpinnings of sparse categorical cross-entropy, illustrating its role in quantifying the model's prediction errors.

Model Training - Orchestrating the Learning Symphony

Training the CNN on spectrogram datasets is akin to conducting an intricate symphony, where each note contributes to the harmonious understanding of audio signals.

Epochs: The Training Cycles

An epoch represents a full cycle through the entire training dataset. Deciding the number of epochs is a balance between sufficient learning and avoiding overfitting. Too few epochs might underfit the model, while too many can lead to overfitting.

EarlyStopping: The Conductor's Pause

Integrate callbacks like EarlyStopping to monitor the model's performance on the validation set. This mechanism halts training when the validation loss ceases to decrease, indicating that the model is no longer learning effectively and is starting to memorize the training data.

The Iterative Dance of Weights and Loss

During training, the model's weights are iteratively adjusted based on the loss function. This function quantifies the difference between the predicted output and the actual label, guiding the model towards greater accuracy.

Validation: The Litmus Test

The validation set, distinct from the training data, provides a reality check for the model's learning. It is crucial for evaluating the model's performance and generalizability to unseen data.

Prediction - Decoding the Unheard

The culmination of the audio recognition model's journey lies in its ability to make predictions. This final act of the model's performance is where the trained CNN applies its learned patterns to unseen data, translating spectrograms into meaningful classifications.

The Art of Inference

Prediction in machine learning is an inference process. The model, now trained, is presented with new spectrogram inputs. These inputs pass through the network's layers, each contributing to the final output: a prediction of the audio's content.

Analyzing the Output

The output of the model is a set of probabilities, each corresponding to a potential class label. The class with the highest probability is typically chosen as the model's prediction. This decision-making process is often accompanied by a confidence score, providing insight into the model's certainty.

Understanding Transfer Learning

Transfer Learning is a revolutionary technique in the world of machine learning, particularly in the realm of audio recognition. It involves taking a model trained on one task and repurposing it for a second, related task. This approach is especially beneficial in scenarios where labeled data is scarce or when training a model from scratch is computationally expensive.

In audio recognition, pre-trained models on vast datasets, such as those identifying generic speech patterns or environmental sounds, serve as a foundational knowledge base. These models, having learned a wide array of audio features, can be fine-tuned with a smaller, task-specific dataset. This process significantly reduces the time and resources required for training while maintaining high accuracy levels.

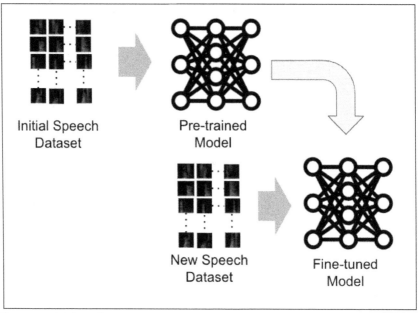

Figure 9.16: Transfer learning example adapting a speech model for new tasks

The essence of transfer learning in audio recognition lies in its ability to adapt. For instance, a model initially trained to recognize words in a speech dataset can be retrained to identify specific sounds in a different environment, like bird songs or urban noises. This adaptation typically involves adjusting the final layers of the neural network to align with the new audio context.

The retraining process usually involves freezing the initial layers of the model, which contain the generalized knowledge, and only training the latter layers. This technique allows the model to maintain its learned features while adapting to new data. Mathematically, this is represented by keeping the weights of the initial layers constant, while updating the weights of the latter layers during the training process.

To implement transfer learning, one typically starts with a robust pre-trained model, such as a Convolutional Neural Network (CNN) trained on a comprehensive audio dataset. The model is then exposed to new audio data, and its final layers are trained to recognize these new sound patterns.

Transfer Learning in Action: Customizing Speech Recognition with TensorFlow.js

This section provides a guided walk-through on how to personalize speech recognition using TensorFlow.js. The process leverages transfer learning to enhance a pre-trained model with custom audio inputs, enabling applications to recognize new spoken commands.

Set Up the Environment

Begin by installing TensorFlow.js in your project environment using one of the following commands:

```
npm install @tensorflow/tfjs
# or
yarn add @tensorflow/tfjs
```

This setup provides the tools necessary for incorporating machine learning features directly in the browser or via Node.js.

Load the Pre-Trained Model

Initialize the base speech recognition model using:

```
const recognizer = speechCommands.create('BROWSER_FFT');
await recognizer.ensureModelLoaded();
```

This loads a model designed to work with Fast Fourier Transform (FFT) features in the browser. The ensureModelLoaded() method guarantees the model's resources are ready before use.

Collect Custom Speech Samples

To add new commands, create a transfer learning model and begin collecting training samples:

```
const transferRecognizer = recognizer.createTransfer('customCommands');
await transferRecognizer.collectExample('yes');
await transferRecognizer.collectExample('no');
await transferRecognizer.collectExample('_background_noise_');
```

Collect multiple examples for each label to improve generalization and include background noise for robustness.

Check the current dataset status with:

```
console.log(transferRecognizer.countExamples());
```

Train the Model on New Data

Use your collected samples to train the transfer recognizer:

```
await transferRecognizer.train({
  epochs: 20,
  callback: {
    onEpochEnd: async (epoch, logs) => {
      console.log(`Epoch ${epoch}: Loss = ${logs.loss}, Accuracy = ${logs.acc}`);
    }
  }
});
```

Here, the epochs value determines how many times the model will iterate over the dataset, while the callback logs training progress.

Recognize Speech in Real Time

Once trained, you can activate real-time speech recognition:

```
await transferRecognizer.listen(result => {
  const scores = result.scores;
  const labels = transferRecognizer.wordLabels();
  const topScoreIndex = scores.indexOf(Math.max(...scores));
  console.log(`Recognized word: ${labels[topScoreIndex]}`);
}, {
  probabilityThreshold: 0.75
});
```

The probabilityThreshold ensures only predictions with high confidence are processed.

Save and Reuse Audio Data

You can serialize collected examples to preserve your dataset or transfer it elsewhere:

```
const serialized = transferRecognizer.serializeExamples();
```

To reload the examples later:

```
await newTransferRecognizer.loadExamples(serialized, true);
```

This allows you to reuse training data across sessions or applications.

Here is the complete program that brings together all the steps outlined above. This script demonstrates how to load a pre-trained speech model, collect custom audio samples, perform transfer learning, and activate real-time recognition using **TensorFlow.js**:

```
import * as speechCommands from '@tensorflow-models/speech-commands';

// Step 1: Load the base model
const recognizer = speechCommands.create('BROWSER_FFT');
await recognizer.ensureModelLoaded();

// Step 2: Create a transfer learning recognizer
const transferRecognizer = recognizer.createTransfer('customCommands');

// Step 3: Collect audio examples for new commands
await transferRecognizer.collectExample('yes');
await transferRecognizer.collectExample('no');
await transferRecognizer.collectExample('_background_noise_');

// Optional: Monitor example counts
console.log(transferRecognizer.countExamples());

// Step 4: Train the model with new samples
await transferRecognizer.train({
  epochs: 20,
  callback: {
    onEpochEnd: async (epoch, logs) => {
      console.log(`Epoch ${epoch + 1}: Loss = ${logs.loss}, Accuracy = ${logs.acc}`);
    }
  }
});

// Step 5: Activate live recognition
await transferRecognizer.listen(result => {
  const scores = result.scores;
  const labels = transferRecognizer.wordLabels();
  const topScoreIndex = scores.indexOf(Math.max(...scores));
  console.log(`Recognized word: ${labels[topScoreIndex]}`);
}, {
  probabilityThreshold: 0.75
});
```

```
// Step 6: Save training data
const serialized = transferRecognizer.serializeExamples();

// Step 7: Load saved data later or in another session
const newTransferRecognizer = recognizer.createTransfer('customCommands');
await newTransferRecognizer.loadExamples(serialized, true);
```

Summary

This chapter explores the intersection of artificial intelligence and audio recognition, focusing on how AI systems process and interpret sound signals. It delves into the mechanisms behind AI's ability to recognize speech, music, and environmental sounds, emphasizing the role of Digital Signal Processing (DSP) and techniques like the Fast Fourier Transform (FFT) in breaking down and analyzing audio spectra. The chapter highlights various applications of audio recognition, including voice authentication, medical diagnostics, virtual assistants, and music analysis. It also explains speech recognition models, the importance of spectrograms, and the use of Convolutional Neural Networks (CNNs) in processing auditory data. Additionally, it covers transfer learning techniques for adapting pre-trained speech models and introduces TensorFlow.js for customizing speech recognition systems in real-world applications.

Chapter 10: Natural Language Processing (NLP)

In the ever-evolving landscape of artificial intelligence (AI), Natural Language Processing (NLP) emerges as a pivotal and captivating field, primarily focusing on equipping computers with the ability to comprehend, interpret, and interact with human language. This domain effectively narrows the divide between human communication and digital data processing, granting machines the proficiency to read, decipher, and react to human languages in a meaningful and constructive manner. Combining elements of computational linguistics, machine learning, and deep learning, NLP is adept at processing and analyzing vast quantities of natural language data. Its diverse applications, ranging from machine translation and speech recognition to sentiment analysis and chatbot interactions, significantly influence various facets of technology and daily life.

Applications of NLP

The applications of NLP are diverse and impact various aspects of technology and daily life. Here are some key applications:

- Machine Translation: NLP enables the translation of text or speech from one language to another, facilitating global communication. This technology underpins popular tools like Google Translate, helping break language barriers in real-time.

- Speech Recognition: This involves converting spoken words into written text. NLP technologies power voice-controlled assistants like Siri and Alexa, enabling them to understand and respond to verbal commands.

- Text Summarization: NLP can condense large volumes of text into concise summaries, retaining key information and context. This is especially useful in digesting news articles, research papers, or lengthy documents.

- Sentiment Analysis: By analyzing the tone and emotional context of text, NLP helps in determining whether the sentiment behind a piece of text is positive, negative, or neutral. This application is widely used in monitoring social media, customer reviews, and market research.

- Spam Detection: NLP aids in filtering out unsolicited or irrelevant messages, especially in email inboxes. It uses pattern recognition and anomaly detection to identify and segregate spam from legitimate communication.

- Question Answering: This involves building systems that can answer questions posed by humans in a natural language. It's a complex task as the system needs to understand the question's context and provide accurate, relevant answers.

- Information Extraction: NLP is used to automatically extract structured information from unstructured text, such as names, dates, and places from news articles or documents. This is crucial in data mining and big data applications.

- Topic Modeling and Categorization: NLP algorithms can determine the main topics or categories within large volumes of text, aiding in organizing and summarizing content for better information retrieval and understanding.

- Chatbots: NLP enables chatbots to interact naturally with humans through text or voice. These bots can provide customer support, answer inquiries, and offer personalized experiences, revolutionizing how businesses engage with customers.

- Language Generation: NLP can generate human-like text based on certain inputs, used in applications like automatic report generation, content creation for websites, and even creative writing.

- Named Entity Recognition (NER): This involves identifying and classifying key information (entities) in text, such as names of people, organizations, locations, expressions of times, quantities, monetary values, and more.

- Part-of-Speech Tagging: NLP is used to identify and tag the part of speech of each word in a text, which is fundamental in understanding sentence structures and grammar in various languages.

- Relationship Extraction: Identifying relationships between named entities in a text, like who works for whom or what a specific product is a part of, is another critical application.

- Semantic Parsing: This involves understanding the meaning and the structure of sentences, crucial for applications like question answering and machine translation.

- Biomedical Text Mining: NLP is applied in the biomedical field for drug discovery, clinical trial matching, and extracting information from electronic health records.

These applications showcase the versatility and breadth of NLP, highlighting its significance in various fields and industries. As NLP continues to evolve with advancements in AI and machine learning, its applications are likely to expand further, offering even more innovative and efficient solutions to complex language-related challenges.

Basics of Language Understanding

Human language is an complex system, composed fundamentally of words, phrases, sentences, and their respective structures. These elements serve as the building blocks of communication. Words, the smallest units with distinct meanings, come together to form phrases. Phrases, a collection of words that express a singular concept, then combine to create sentences – the primary structures for expressing complete thoughts.

For instance, consider the sentence "The cat sat on the mat." Here, "the cat" and "on the mat" are phrases that contribute to the overall meaning of the sentence. The sentence structure allows us to convey a specific idea or action, in this case, what the cat is doing and where. Understanding this hierarchical structure of language is crucial in grasping how meaning is formed and communicated.

Understanding Syntax

Syntax refers to the set of rules, principles, and processes that govern the structure of sentences in a language. It is essentially about the arrangement of words and phrases to create well-formed, grammatically correct sentences.

Syntax is not about the meaning of words themselves but how words are combined.

For example, in English, a simple syntactic rule is that a typical sentence follows a Subject-Verb-Object structure. So, "The dog chased the ball" follows this syntax, whereas "Chased the ball the dog" does not. NLP systems use these syntactic rules to parse and understand sentences. By analyzing the syntax, NLP systems can determine which words are serving as subjects, objects, verbs, and so on, helping the system understand the basic structure of the input language.

The Role of Semantics

While syntax is about structure, semantics is about meaning. Semantics in NLP deals with understanding the meanings of words and how these meanings combine in sentences to form the meanings of sentences. It involves interpreting the connotations and implications of words and sentences beyond their literal definitions.

Semantics is crucial in NLP for grasping the nuances of language. For instance, the word "bank" can mean the edge of a river or a financial institution, depending on the context. NLP systems use semantic analysis to discern these differences, allowing them to understand the intended meaning in different contexts. This understanding is key to applications like machine translation or voice recognition, where the context determines the correct interpretation.

Grammar and Punctuation in NLP

Grammar and punctuation play significant roles in language understanding. Grammar rules help determine how words combine to form valid sentences, while punctuation marks aid in understanding the structure and rhythm of sentences.

In NLP, grammar and punctuation are used to better understand the structure and meaning of text. For example, the presence of a question mark at the end of a sentence signals that the sentence is a question, which can change how an NLP system interprets the sentence's meaning. Similarly, the use of commas can change the meaning of a sentence, as in "Let's eat, grandma" versus "Let's eat grandma."

NLP systems are programmed to recognize and interpret these grammatical rules and punctuation marks. This ability helps them parse sentences accurately, understand the context, and respond appropriately in applications like text-to-speech conversion or automated grammar checking.

From Text to Meaning

The journey of understanding human language for an NLP system begins with text recognition. This process involves the identification and conversion of written or spoken language into a format that machines can process.

Breaking Down Language

Once text is recognized and input into the system, the next step is breaking it down into smaller, more manageable units. This process involves parsing sentences into words and phrases and is a crucial step in understanding the structure of the language.

For example, consider the sentence "The quick brown fox jumps over the lazy dog." An NLP system breaks this down into individual words ("The", "quick", "brown", "fox", etc.) and phrases. This breakdown helps the system analyze the sentence's structure, identify parts of speech, and prepare for deeper levels of understanding.

Context and Word Meanings

One of the significant challenges in language processing is understanding the context to accurately interpret word meanings, especially for words with multiple meanings.

Take the word "bat," which can mean a piece of sports equipment or a nocturnal mammal. In the sentence "I saw a bat flying at night," the context makes it clear that "bat" refers to the animal. NLP systems use similar contextual clues to infer the correct meanings of words in various situations.

Understanding Sentences and Paragraphs

Beyond individual words and phrases, NLP systems also focus on understanding the larger structure and meaning of sentences and paragraphs.

This involves recognizing the relationships between words, the flow of ideas, and the overall theme.

For instance, in a paragraph describing a beach, the system identifies descriptive words (like "sandy," "sunny," "waves") and understands that these words collectively describe a location. Understanding sentence structure and paragraph themes allows NLP systems to grasp the broader context and meaning, which is essential in applications like text summarization or reading comprehension.

Practical Examples

Spam Detection

Spam detection is one of the most common and impactful applications of Natural Language Processing (NLP) in our digital lives. It primarily focuses on identifying and filtering out unsolicited or irrelevant messages, particularly in email communication. The process involves sophisticated pattern recognition and anomaly detection techniques that are hallmark capabilities of NLP.

The fundamental operation of spam detection using NLP involves analyzing the content of emails. The system scans the text for known spam indicators, which can include specific words, phrases, or patterns commonly found in spam emails. For instance, phrases like "You won a lottery!" or "Urgent money transfer required" are typical markers that a message might be spam.

NLP systems also learn from new data, adapting to the ever-evolving tactics of spammers. Machine learning models, a subset of NLP, are trained on large datasets of both spam and legitimate emails. These models learn to distinguish between the two by recognizing subtle patterns and anomalies that might not be immediately obvious to human readers.

Moreover, NLP-based spam filters don't just look at the text. They analyze the email's metadata, such as the sender's information, sending patterns, and the frequency of emails sent to multiple recipients. This holistic approach enhances the accuracy of spam detection, ensuring that important, legitimate emails are less likely to be incorrectly marked as spam.

Example 1:

Below is an example of how the "Spam Detection" pre-trained model operates within the realm of Natural Language Processing. The model, designed to classify sentences as spam or not, demonstrates its efficacy through two distinct prediction examples. In the first, a seemingly promotional message is accurately categorized as spam, while in the second, a genuine comment is appropriately recognized as not-spam. This showcases the model's precision and adaptability in analyzing and interpreting diverse textual inputs, a critical attribute for effective spam detection in various digital communication contexts.

Pre-trained Model:

Name	Spam Detection
Description	Classifies a comment sentence as spam or no-spam
Type	NLP classification
Homepage	https://www.kaggle.com/models/ tensorflow/spamdetection/frameworks/tfJs/ variations/tfjs/versions/1
Total Parameters	14093
Input limit	20 words max

Figure 10.1: Overview of the Spam Detection model architecture

In the above description of the "Spam Detection" model, we see a concise summary of its capabilities and specifications. Classified as an NLP classification type, this model is adept at determining whether a given sentence, particularly a comment, is spam or not. Its architecture, suitable for handling short texts up to 20 words, is ideal for quick and efficient spam filtering in online communication platforms. The model is accessible through its Kaggle homepage, offering insights into its framework and variations.

Model Summary:

The following model summary provides a detailed look at the architecture of the Spam Detection model. Starting with an input layer designed for a maximum of 20 words, it uses an embedding layer with 14,021 parameters to process and understand the textual input. The global average pooling and dense layers further analyze the embedded text, with a dropout layer for regularization. The final dense layer, consisting of 2 units, classifies the input into 'Spam' or 'Not-Spam'. The model's design, with a total of 14,093 parameters, is optimized for efficient processing and accurate spam detection.

Layer (type)	Output shape	Param #
input_1 (**InputLayer**)	[null,20]	0
embedding (**Embedding**)	[null,20, 7]	14021
global_average_pooling1d (**GlobalAverage**)	[null, 7]	0
dense (**Dense**)	[null, 7]	56
dropout (**Dropout**)	[null, 7]	0
dense_1 (**Dense**)	[null, 2]	16

Total params: **14093**
Trainable params: **14093**
Non-trainable params: **0**

In the first prediction example of the model, the input sentence "Nice article, check out my website for amazing deals on shoes!" is tokenized into a series of numerical values, where each word is mapped to a unique integer based on a predefined vocabulary created during training. This transformation allows the model to process the sentence numerically. The numbers correspond to the index of each word in the tokenizer's vocabulary. The trailing zeros indicate padding — extra values added to reach a fixed input length expected by the model. Padding ensures all input sequences have uniform length, which is crucial for consistent model input and efficient computation. The model's output assigns a high probability of 0.979 to the sentence being spam, illustrating its capability to identify promotional or unsolicited content effectively.

Input	Nice article, check out my website for amazing deals on shoes!
Input - tokenized	1,33,58,2,83,1938,146,20,531,445,1287,749,2,2,0,0,0,0,0,0
Output **(probability)**	Not-Spam: 0.021 Spam: 0.979

Figure 10.2: Spam prediction example showing model analysis

Example 2:

The second prediction example demonstrates the model's nuanced understanding. The input "I am leaving this comment with genuine interest" is processed and tokenized similarly. However, the model's output shows a higher probability (0.728) of the sentence being not-spam, highlighting the model's ability to discern genuine comments from spam effectively.

Input	I am leaving this comment with genuine interest.
Input-tokenized	1,3,2,618,51,582,1769,2,653,2,0,0,0,0,0,0,0,0,0,0
Output (probability)	Not-Spam: 0.728 Spam: 0.272

Figure 10.3: Comment classified accurately as not-spam.

The above Spam Detection example effectively demonstrates the robust capabilities of the pre-trained NLP classification model. It emphasizes how the model, with its intricate architecture capable of processing up to 20 words, excels in distinguishing between spam and legitimate messages. This is evidenced by its precise analysis of different types of input sentences – one promotional and the other genuine – and its ability to classify them accurately as spam and not-spam respectively. Such efficiency and accuracy, powered by 14,093 parameters including an embedding layer and dense layers, underscore the model's utility in enhancing spam filtering processes across online communication platforms.

Question Answering

Question answering systems represent a more complex and interactive application of NLP. These systems are designed to comprehend questions posed in natural language and provide accurate, contextually relevant answers.

The process involves several steps, starting with parsing the question to understand its structure and intent. The system breaks down the question into key components – often identifying the subject, object, and other critical elements of the query.

Once the question is analyzed, the system searches its knowledge base or the internet for information relevant to the question. This search process is not just about finding keywords but understanding the context and nuance of the question. For example, if someone asks, "What's the tallest building in the world?" the system needs to recognize that the answer should be a building's name and its height.

The final step is generating an answer. In some cases, this might involve simply retrieving a piece of information, like in the example above. In more complex scenarios, the system might need to synthesize information from multiple sources or perform calculations.

Question answering systems are increasingly sophisticated, often employing advanced AI models like deep learning to improve understanding and response accuracy. They are widely used in virtual assistants, customer service chatbots, and information retrieval systems, making information access more efficient and user-friendly.

Below is an example of how the "Question and Answer" pre-trained model adeptly navigates through the details of Nikola Tesla's life, as outlined in the provided context. The model, leveraging its advanced NLP capabilities, accurately pinpoints and prioritizes answers to queries about Tesla's birthplace, his renowned achievements, and educational background. This demonstrates not only the model's ability to sift through and analyze extensive textual information but also its skill in discerning and presenting the most pertinent facts in response to specific questions, exemplifying the cutting-edge advancements in the realm of NLP-driven question-answering systems.

Name	Question and Answer
Description	Answers questions based on the content of a given passage.
Type	NLP classification
Homepage	https://www.kaggle.com/models/tensorflow/ spamdetection/frameworks/tfJs/variations/ tfjs/versions/1
Total Parameters	14093
Input limit	20 words max

Figure 10.4: Question Answer model setup for NLP applications

In the above description of the "Question and Answer" model, we see an overview of its purpose and design. This model, categorized under NLP Question Answering, is tailored to provide answers based on a given text passage. Utilizing the MobileBERT language model, which has been fine-tuned on the SQuAD 2.0 dataset, it demonstrates a remarkable ability to comprehend and extract specific information from a predefined context. The model, accessible via its homepage, is a prime example of advanced NLP applications in the field of knowledge extraction and automated question-answering systems.

The following context provided to the "Question and Answer" model offers a comprehensive overview of Nikola Tesla's life and achievements. It details Tesla's background as a Serbian-American inventor, his significant contributions to the AC electricity supply system, and his journey through various phases of his career, from working in telephony and electric power to his experiments with wireless communication and power transmission. This rich and detailed narrative sets the stage for the model to demonstrate its capabilities in accurately answering questions related to Tesla's life and work.

Predefined Context

Nikola Tesla was a Serbian-American inventor, electrical engineer, mechanical engineer, and futurist who is best known for his contributions to the design of the modern alternating current (AC) electricity supply system.

Born and raised in the Austrian Empire, Tesla studied engineering and physics in the 1870s without receiving a degree, and gained practical experience in the early 1880s working in telephony and at Continental Edison in the new electric power industry. He emigrated in 1884 to the United States, where he would become a naturalized citizen. He worked for a short time at the Edison Machine Works in New York City before he struck out on his own. With the help of partners to finance and market his ideas, Tesla set up laboratories and companies in New York to develop a range of electrical and mechanical devices. His alternating current (AC) induction motor and related polyphase AC patents, licensed by Westinghouse Electric in 1888, earned him a considerable amount of money and became the cornerstone of the polyphase system which that company would eventually market.

Attempting to develop inventions he could patent and market, Tesla conducted a range of experiments with mechanical oscillators/generators, electrical discharge tubes, and early X-ray imaging. He also built a wireless-controlled boat, one of the first ever exhibited. Tesla became well known as an inventor and would demonstrate his achievements to celebrities and wealthy patrons at his lab, and was noted for his showmanship at public lectures. Throughout the 1890s, Tesla pursued his ideas for wireless lighting and worldwide wireless electric power distribution in his high-voltage, high-frequency power experiments in New York and Colorado Springs. In 1893, he made pronouncements on the possibility of wireless communication with his devices. Tesla tried to put these ideas to practical use in his unfinished Wardenclyffe Tower project, an intercontinental wireless communication and power transmitter, but ran out of funding before he could complete it.

After Wardenclyffe, Tesla experimented with a series of inventions in the 1910s and 1920s with varying degrees of success. Having spent most of his money, Tesla lived in a series of New York hotels, leaving behind unpaid bills. He died in New York City in January 1943. Tesla's work fell into relative obscurity following his death, until 1960, when the General Conference on Weights and Measures named the SI unit of magnetic flux density the tesla in his honor. There has been a resurgence in popular interest in Tesla since the 1990s.

Below is an example of how the "Question and Answer" pre-trained model functions in the context of the provided information about Nikola Tesla. When posed with specific questions about Tesla's birthplace, his fame, and his academic background, the model successfully identifies and ranks relevant answers with corresponding scores. These responses, derived from the detailed context, showcase the model's proficiency in comprehending complex text and extracting precise and relevant information, reflecting the advanced state of NLP in question-answering applications.

Question	Answers (top 3)	Score
Where Tesla was born?	Austrian Empire	20.32
	the Austrian Empire	14.17
	Austrian	12.58
What Tesla was famous for?	inventor	15.77
	his contributions to the design of the	14.72

	modern alternating current (AC) electricity supply system	
	contributions to the design of the modern alternating current (AC) electricity supply system	11.23
What did he study?	engineering and physics	24.79
	studied engineering and physics	13.24
	engineering and physics in the 1870s without receiving a degree	12.66

Figure 10.5: Extracting answers using the Question Answer model

The above Question/Answer example with the pre-trained model illustrates its impressive capability in extracting precise answers from a complex textual context. The model, utilizing its advanced NLP framework, adeptly navigates through a detailed narrative of Nikola Tesla's life, responding accurately to questions about his birthplace, famed contributions, and educational background.

Language Modeling

In the expansive field of Natural Language Processing (NLP), Language Modeling stands as a cornerstone, directly contributing to the broader objective of Language Understanding and Analysis. It forms the foundational layer upon which various complex NLP tasks are built, ranging from speech recognition to text generation. Understanding Language Modeling is essential for comprehending how AI systems process, interpret, and generate human language. At its core, Language Modeling involves predicting the likelihood of a sequence of words. This predictive model calculates the probability of a word or a sequence of words appearing within a given context. The essence of language modeling lies in its ability to capture the patterns and structures of language, thereby facilitating a deeper understanding of linguistic norms and nuances. Language Modeling is integral to understanding both the syntax and semantics of language. By analyzing large text corpora, language models learn not just the frequency of word occurrence but also their typical placements and associations within sentences. This knowledge allows for the prediction of subsequent words in a sentence, thereby aiding in the comprehension of language structure and flow.

Types of Language Models

Below are the various types of language models, each representing a significant stage in the evolution of NLP:

- **Statistical Language Models**: Earlier models relied on statistical methods, using the frequency and occurrence of words to predict the next word in a sequence. These include n-gram models and Markov models, which were foundational in early NLP applications.

- **Neural Network-Based Models**: More recently, neural networks have revolutionized language modeling. These models, including Recurrent Neural Networks (RNNs) and Long Short-Term Memory (LSTM) networks, can capture longer-range dependencies and subtler linguistic patterns, leading to more accurate predictions.

- **Transformers and Bidirectional Models**: The advent of models like BERT (Bidirectional Encoder Representations from Transformers) introduced bidirectional context understanding, allowing for even more nuanced language understanding. These models process text in both directions (left-to-right and right-to-left), offering a comprehensive context analysis.

Transformers and Bidirectional Models

The field of Natural Language Processing (NLP) has witnessed a paradigm shift with the advent of Transformer models and their bidirectional counterparts, such as BERT (Bidirectional Encoder Representations from Transformers). These models have redefined the approach to Language Modeling, enabling a deeper, more nuanced understanding of language context. They represent a significant evolution from traditional models, processing text in a way that captures the full extent of linguistic context.

The introduction of Transformer models marked a departure from conventional neural network architectures used in NLP, like Recurrent Neural Networks (RNNs) and Long Short-Term Memory (LSTM) networks. Unlike their predecessors, which processed text sequentially (either from left-to-right or right-to-left), Transformer models utilize a mechanism known as self-attention. This allows them to process entire sequences of text simultaneously, considering each word in the context of all others in the sentence, leading to a more holistic understanding of text.

Applications of Transformer Models

The capabilities of Transformer models have broadened the scope of possible applications in NLP. These include but are not limited to:

- Machine Translation: Achieving more accurate translations due to a better understanding of context.
- Sentiment Analysis: More accurately determining the sentiment of texts by understanding the nuances of language.
- Question Answering: Providing precise answers by comprehensively analyzing the context of both questions and possible answers.
- Text Summarization: Creating more coherent and contextually relevant summaries of large texts.

Advantages Over Previous Models

Transformers and bidirectional models offer several advantages over traditional language models:

- Efficiency: They are more efficient as they process entire text sequences at once, unlike RNNs and LSTMs which process word-by-word.
- Contextual Accuracy: Their ability to consider full context results in a more accurate understanding of language.
- Flexibility: These models can be fine-tuned for a wide range of specific NLP tasks.

The Architecture of Transformer Model

The introduction of Transformers and Bidirectional Models like BERT in Natural Language Processing (NLP) has brought forward several key concepts that are foundational to their success. Among these, Word Embedding, Position Embedding, and Attention Score stand out as crucial elements that enable these models to process and understand language in a sophisticated manner. These concepts are interlinked and work in tandem to enhance the language understanding capabilities of Transformers.

Word Embedding

Word Embedding is a technique in NLP where words or phrases from the vocabulary are mapped to vectors of real numbers, effectively translating text into a form that can be understood by machine learning algorithms. Unlike traditional word embeddings that give a single representation per word, models like BERT provide 'contextual embeddings'. This means the same word can have different representations based on its context within a sentence, leading to more context-aware language understanding.

Let's consider a very simple example of word embedding in vector form, as shown in the table below, with three columns labeled "Gender", "Age", and "Royalty".

	Gender	Age	Royalty
grandfather	-0.54	0.64	-0.54
man	-0.72	0.46	-0.52
woman	0.77	0.42	-0.48
boy	-0.7	-0.51	-0.51
girl	0.75	-0.46	-0.46
king	-0.46	0.51	0.66
monarch	0.07	0.47	0.88
queen	0.66	0.36	0.66
prince	-0.58	-0.43	0.69
princess	0.65	-0.4	0.65
child	0.07	-0.59	-0.81
infant	0.06	-0.71	-0.71

Figure 10.6: Simple word embedding example in three dimensions

These columns represent the different dimensions or attributes of the words listed in the rows of the table. These rows list different words such as "grandfather," "man," "woman," and so on. Each word in a row has corresponding values in the three columns, providing a numerical representation for that word in terms of its gender, age, and royalty attributes. These numeric values are the components of the embedding vector. This is an example of word embedding in 3 dimensions and is provided for understanding the concept. In real NLP systems, the dimension of the word embedding vector can be in the hundreds.

Let's analyze each of the dimensions in this word embedding example. For the gender dimension, positive values indicate femininity, while negative values indicate masculinity. For example, "woman" has a value of 0.77, indicating strong femininity, while "man" has a value of -0.72, indicating strong masculinity. Gender-neutral words such as "monarch" will have values close to zero, such as 0.07, indicating gender neutrality.

For the Age dimension, positive values represent older age and negative values represent youth. The word "grandfather" has a value of 0.64, indicating older age, while "infant" has a value of -0.71, indicating very young age.

For the royalty dimension, positive values indicate royal status, while negative values indicate non-royalty. The word "monarch" has a high value of 0.88, indicating strong royal status, while "child" has a value of -0.81, indicating a lack of royal association.

Essentially, these vectors provide a numerical representation of the characteristics of each word. For example, "queen" has positive values in both gender and royalty, indicating that it's associated with femininity and royalty. On the other hand, "boy" has negative values on all dimensions, suggesting masculinity, youth, and non-royalty.

Next, we can visualize these embedding vectors in 3D by plotting the word embedding vectors as a 3D scatterplot, as shown below.

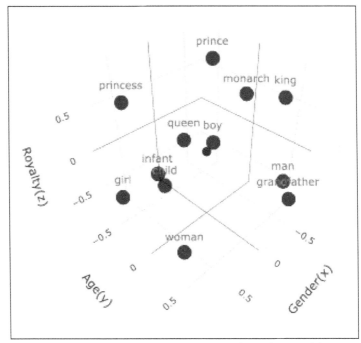

Figure 10.7: D scatterplot visualization of word embeddings

In this plot, each embedding vector is represented by a dot, with the gender, age, and royalty components on the x, y, and z axes, respectively, and the origin shown as a smaller dot. By visually inspecting these words in 3D space, we can see if and in what aspects the two words are close to each other.

Position Embedding

One of the unique aspects of Transformers is their non-sequential processing of text. However, the order of words in a sentence carries essential meaning, which brings us to Position Embedding. The Position Embeddings are added to word embeddings to give the model information about the position of words in a sentence. This allows the Transformer to understand the order of words, a crucial aspect of language structure. Some advanced models use 'relative' position embeddings to understand the relative positions of words to each other, further enhancing the model's ability to capture contextual nuances.

The most widely used representation of position embedding consists of multiple sine and cosine waves as shown in the below image. This representation offers a continuous and unique encoding for each word position. The periodic nature of sine and cosine functions allows the model to capture both short-term and long-term positional relationships.

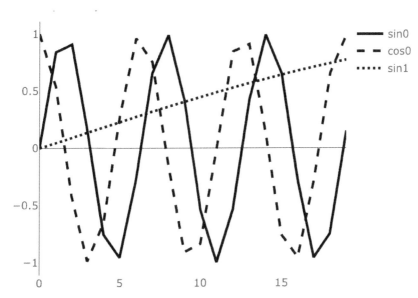

Figure 10.8: Position embedding using sine and cosine waves

Here is the formula to calculate the sine and cosine values:

$$PE(p, 2i) = \sin\left(\frac{p}{n^{\frac{2i}{d}}}\right)$$

$$PE(p, 2i + 1) = \cos\left(\frac{p}{n^{\frac{2i}{d}}}\right)$$

$$\text{where} \quad 0 \leq p < L$$
$$0 \leq i < d/2$$

Where:

- d is the total embedding dimension.

- n is the Frequency Factor (which is generally equal to 10000 for real-life systems).

- p represents the position of a token (word) within the sequence.

- i represents the dimension of the embedding. Given that the embedding has a total dimension of d, i can take values from 1 up to

$$d/2$$

- PE(p,i) is the position embedding of position p at dimension i

- The terms 2i and 2i+1 ensure that sine is applied to the even dimensions and cosine to the odd dimensions.

We use the following values of d, n and p to calculate the sine and cosine values shown in the above image.

$$d = 3$$
$$n = 100$$
$$L = 20$$

To illustrate the position embedding process, the model applies specific values: $d=3$, $n=100$, and L=20, ss shown in Figure 10.8. In this context, d represents the embedding dimension, meaning that for each token position, three values are generated—one for each dimension. The frequency factor $n=100$ scales the sine and cosine functions to control their periodicity, while $L=20$ defines the sequence length, resulting in embeddings for 20 token positions. According to the equations, sine is applied to even-numbered dimensions (e.g., 0 and 2) and cosine to odd-numbered dimensions (e.g., 1). The curves in Figure 10.8 demonstrate how this approach encodes each token's position with smoothly varying signals, enabling the model to capture both short- and long-range dependencies in the input sequence.

To plot the graphs, we start with i=0 and calculate sin and call it **sine0** which is plotted as **solid line** then we calculate cos for i=0 and call it **cos0**, plotted as **long-dotted line**. Then we increment i to 1 and calculate sin and call it **sin1**, plotted as the **short-dotted line**. This way we have covered all 3 dimensions of the embedding space. The x-axis of this frequency plot is the position p of a token or word; this value starts from 0 and goes up to the sequence length L.

The overall positional embedding value of a token or word is the net value of all the sine and cosine components. This net or overall position embedding (or value) of a word can also be represented as a 3D scatter chart as shown in the below image.

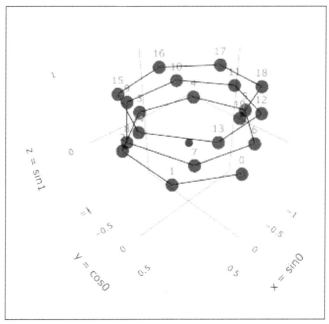

Figure 10.9: 3D scatter chart of positional embeddings for sequence tokens

In this chart the circle 0 is the positional embedding when a word is at position 0, the circle 1 is the position embedding when a word is at position 1 and so on. This visualization reveals a spiral-like pattern formed by the positional embeddings, with each position wrapping around the previous one. As the position index increases, the corresponding embedding traces an outward and upward path in 3D space, illustrating how the model encodes sequential progression through continuous and structured changes in the embedding representation.

Segment Embedding

Segment Embedding is an important component in the BERT architecture that enables the model to distinguish between different segments of input text. In tasks such as Next Sentence Prediction (NSP), where the model must determine if one sentence logically follows another, understanding which parts of the input belong to separate text segments becomes essential.

In BERT, input samples can contain up to two segments. To help the model differentiate between these, Segment IDs are used. These IDs are assigned to each token in the input, with the values 0 and 1 representing the first and second segments, respectively. By associating each token with a segment ID, the model can understand the separation and relationships between different parts of the text.

Attention Score

The Attention mechanism is arguably the most critical innovation in Transformers, enabling these models to focus on different parts of the input sequence when performing a task. There are two types of attention score:

- Self-Attention: In Transformer models, the self-attention mechanism allows each word in the input sequence to attend to all other words. This mechanism calculates an 'Attention Score' for each word pair, determining how much focus to put on other parts of the input when processing a particular word.

- Scaled Dot-Product Attention: This is a specific type of attention used in Transformers. It computes scores based on the dot product of the query (a representation of a word) with all keys (representations of all words in the sequence), which are then scaled, passed through a softmax function, and multiplied with the value (another representation of the word). This process results in a weighted representation that combines information from relevant parts of the input.

As a foundational concept, it's helpful to first understand how a basic attention mechanism operates in scalar form before exploring vector-based attention systems. This helps in building an intuitive grasp of how words are assigned relevance scores based on query-key relationships. In the below image, we observe an example of a scalar-based attention scoring system. It depicts a straightforward mapping where keys such as "apple," "banana," and "chair" are associated with scalar values 9, 6, and 3, respectively.

Key	Value
apple	9
banana	6
chair	3

Figure 10.10: Mapping keys to values in a scalar data structure

Queries:

Key: apple ⇒ Value: 9 (probability=1.0)

Key: banana ⇒ Value: 6 (probability=1.0)

Key: chair ⇒ value: 3 (probability=1.0)

Key: fruit ⇒ value: **? (probability=?)**

When queries for these specific keys are made, the system returns the associated value with absolute certainty; however, it falls short when a query like "fruit" is issued, as it cannot extrapolate from the existing keys.

Figure 10.11 introduces a vector-based attention scoring model where each entity—namely "apple," "banana," and "chair"—is represented using vectors of descriptive attributes. The table displays how these entities are encoded: the first half shows their values across three key features—Sweetness, Durability, and Texture—while the second half presents identical vectors reused for the Value entries, illustrating a scenario where the keys and values are the same. This format helps visualize how attention mechanisms evaluate relationships in a multi-dimensional space. For instance, "apple" scores highest on Sweetness but low on Durability, while "chair" exhibits the opposite pattern. These vector representations form the basis for computing attention weights in a more contextually rich manner, simulating how real models use embeddings to learn and represent semantic relationships between tokens.

	Key			Value		
	Sweetness	Durability	Texture	Sweetness	Durability	Texture
apple	0.9	0.1	0.3	0.9	0.1	0.3
banana	0.7	0.2	0.4	0.7	0.2	0.4
chair	0.1	0.9	0.2	0.1	0.9	0.2

Figure 10.11: Mapping keys to values in a vector data structure

Now, if we want to run a query on this system and this time the query is not a single word or value but rather a vector of values in terms of Sweetness, Durability, and Texture as shown below. In other words we are asking to match keys and values where Sweetness is equal to 0.8, Durability is equal to 0.2 and Texture is equal to 0.1.

Query:

Sweetness: 0.8, Durability: 0.2, Texture: 0.1

Let's assume that we have some system of calculating the 'matching score' between the Query attributes and the Key attributes for each of the entity apple, banana, and chair and this matching score comes out be the below values:

Entity	'Matching score'
apple	0.44
banana	0.37
chair	0.16

Figure 10.12: Entities ranked by their
matching scores

Please notice the top match for this query is apple with a matching score of 0.44 which is higher than 0.37 and 0.16. This 'matching score' is called the Scaled Dot Product and it is computed using the below formula.

$$\textbf{Scaled Dot Product} = \frac{K \cdot Q}{\sqrt{d_k}}$$

- K·Q is the dot product of vectors K and Q.

- dk is the dimensionality of the K vector.

- The scaling by square of dk is done to prevent the dot product from growing too large in magnitude.

In other words, the scaled dot product is the result of taking the dot product between two vectors, K and Q, and then dividing it by the square root of the dimensionality of the vectors. The scaled dot product measures the similarity between two vectors, K and Q, while accounting for their dimensionality. The below table shows the scaled dot product for apple, banana and chair are calculated for the query (0.8, 0.2, 0.1).

dk = 3

Entity	K	Q	$K.Q$	$\dfrac{K \cdot Q}{\sqrt{d_k}}$
apple	$(0.9, 0.1, 0.3)$	$(0.8, 0.2, 0.1)$	$(0.9*0.8+0.1*0.2+0.3*0.1)$ $= \mathbf{0.77}$	0.44
banana	$(0.7, 0.2, 0.4)$	$(0.8, 0.2, 0.1)$	$(0.7*0.8+0.2*0.2+0.4*0.1)$ $= \mathbf{0.64}$	0.37
chair	$(0.1, 0.9, 0.2)$	$(0.8, 0.2, 0.1)$	$(0.1*0.8+0.9*0.2+0.2*0.1)$ $= \mathbf{0.28}$	0.16

Figure 10.13: Calculating the attention scores using K, Q vectors

Now having established the methodology for calculating the scaled dot product, which effectively measures the alignment between query and key vectors in our attention mechanism, we now proceed to refine this raw alignment into a form suitable for probabilistic interpretation. This is where the softmax function comes into play. By applying softmax to the scaled dot products, we transform these raw scores into a distribution of probabilities, thereby enabling the model to discern and assign greater weight to the most relevant inputs. Below is the formula to calculate the Softmax values:

$$\mathbf{Softmax}(x_i) = \frac{e^{x_i}}{\sum_{j=1}^{N} e^{x_j}}$$

where

- x_i is the ith element of the vector x
- e is the base of the natural logarithm.
- The denominator is the sum of the exponential values of all elements in the vector,

If we want to apply the Softmax function to the Scaled Dot product values, the x_i becomes (as previously shown):

$$x_i = \mathbf{Scaled\ Dot\ Product} = \frac{K \cdot Q}{\sqrt{d_k}}$$

Entity	x_i	e^{x_i}	Softmax
apple	0.44	1.553	0.37
banana	0.37	1.448	0.35
chair	0.16	1.174	0.28
Σ		4.175	1.00

Figure 10.14: Calculating the Softmax function

These Softmax values represent the matching score as probabilities between the K and the Q vectors.

Now after having transformed the scaled dot product into a probabilistic distribution via the softmax function, we are now ready to compute the scaled dot product attention. This next computational phase is crucial: it involves multiplying the softmax-normalized weights by the vector of values V. This operation is not just arithmetic, but a synthesis of relevance-the softmax probabilities serve as a weighting system that emphasizes certain features while attenuating others, depending on their computed importance from the softmax stage. By elementwise multiplying these weights with the corresponding values in V, we effectively assemble a weighted sum that epitomizes "attention". This resulting vector is a distilled essence of the input information, attentively modulated to emphasize the most relevant aspects as dictated by the query and is called Scaled Dot Product Attention. We calculate this score using the below formula.

$$\textbf{Attention Score} = \textbf{Softmax}\left(\frac{K \cdot Q}{\sqrt{d_k}}\right) \times V$$

By using the Softmax values calculated in the previous step, we compute the Scaled Product Attention score in the below table.

Entity	Softmax	V	Attention Score
apple	0.37	(0.9, 0.1, 0.3)	(0.33, 0.04, 0.11)
banana	0.35	(0.7, 0.2, 0.4)	(0.24, 0.07, 0.14)
chair	0.28	(0.1, 0.9, 0.2)	(0.03, 0.25, 0.06)

Figure 10.15: Combining Softmax values
with Vectors to derive Attention Scores

In the context of our illustrative example featuring 'apple', 'banana', and 'chair', each with their corresponding key (K) and value (V) vectors, the Scaled Dot Product Attention plays a crucial role. For a given query vector (Q), which may represent a particular fruit's desired characteristics, the dot product attention mechanism efficiently identifies and amplifies the attributes of 'apple' or 'banana' that most closely align with Q. By computing the dot product between Q and each K, and subsequently scaling and normalizing these scores through softmax, we obtain a refined focus on the most relevant entity. Multiplying this focused distribution by V yields an aggregated output that preserves the most salient features corresponding to the query, effectively enabling the Transformer model to 'attend' to the most pertinent information.

BERT: A breakthrough in NLP

BERT, which stands for Bidirectional Encoder Representations from Transformers, is a revolutionary model in natural language processing (NLP). Unlike traditional models that read text in one direction (either left-to-right or right-to-left), BERT analyzes text bidirectionally, capturing the context from both sides of a word. This bidirectional approach allows BERT to better understand the shades of meaning and semantics of words in a sentence. Imagine reading a book and understanding the meaning of a word not only from the words that precede it, but also from the words that follow it. That's the magic of BERT! Its architecture is based on the concept of transformers, which use attention scores to weigh the importance of different words in a sentence. This attention mechanism helps the model focus on words that are more relevant in each context. BERT's capabilities have led to breakthroughs in several NLP tasks such as question answering and spam detection. Its ability to understand the context of words in a sentence makes it exceptionally powerful, and its pre-trained models can be fine-tuned for specific tasks, saving time and computational resources.

The Architecture of BERT

The BERT architecture represents a paradigm shift in natural language processing, leveraging the power of deep learning to understand the nuances and context of human language. The below diagram showcases the inner workings of BERT, beginning at the base with the input text, which in this example is a masked sentence: "The [MASK] chased the mouse. It was a fast

[MASK]." This input text is first converted into input embeddings, which are vectorized representations of the words that encapsulate semantic meaning.

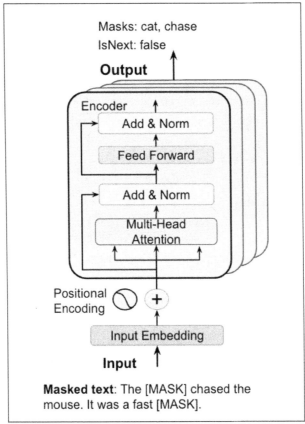

Figure 10.16: Encoder architecture with multi-head
attention for masked text processing

To these input embeddings, positional encodings are added, ensuring that the model retains information about the order of words—a critical aspect of understanding language. The resulting vectors are then passed through a series of encoding layers, each consisting of two sub-layers: a multi-head attention mechanism and a feed-forward neural network, with each sub-layer followed by an "Add & Norm" step that includes residual connections and layer normalization.

The multi-head attention mechanism within the encoder is a distinctive feature of BERT, allowing the model to attend to different parts of the input sentence simultaneously. This mechanism can capture a broad range of contextual clues from all positions in the input sequence, enabling true bidirectionality in understanding language. By using multiple 'heads', BERT can focus on various aspects of language, such as syntax and semantics, concurrently, leading to a rich and nuanced representation of text.

Following each multi-head attention block, the "Add & Norm" step applies a residual connection, which helps in combating the vanishing gradients problem by allowing gradients to flow through the network directly. Layer normalization is also applied to stabilize the learning process, ensuring that the activations don't reach extreme values that could hamper the learning.

The feed-forward network is the second sub-layer of each encoder, introducing additional non-linear transformations that allow BERT to learn complex representations. The output of the feed-forward network is also normalized using an "Add & Norm" step.

As the information flows through the stack of encoders, BERT develops a deep understanding of the input text by considering both the left and right context of each word (or masked token). This is in contrast to previous models that processed text in a unidirectional manner, thereby missing out on the full context.

In the diagram, the top encoder outputs the final representation of the input text, which can then be used for various downstream tasks such as sentiment analysis, question answering, and language inference. The "Masks" notation indicates words that are deliberately hidden during training to encourage the model to predict them based on context. The "IsNext" label refers to a binary prediction task during BERT's pre-training that determines whether two text segments naturally follow each other, which further aids in understanding sentence relationships.

BERT's Pre-Training with MLM and NSP

BERT's pre-training involves two innovative strategies: Masked Language Model (MLM) and Next Sentence Prediction (NSP). These strategies enable the model to understand language context and relationships between sentences.

Masked Language Model (MLM):

During the MLM pre-training task, a certain percentage of the input tokens are randomly masked. For instance, in the sentence "The quick brown fox jumps over the lazy dog," words like "brown" and "over" might be replaced with a [MASK] token, resulting in "The quick [MASK] fox jumps [MASK] the lazy dog." BERT then attempts to predict the original value of the masked words, based solely on their context. This forces the model to develop a deep understanding of the language, as it cannot rely on the left-to-right or right-to-left context only (as was common in previous models) but must use the full context of the surrounding words to make its predictions. Typically, 15% of the words in each sequence are masked during training.

Next Sentence Prediction (NSP):

The NSP task is designed to help BERT understand the relationships between consecutive sentences, which is important for tasks that require understanding the relationship between sentences, such as question answering and natural language inference. During pre-training, the model is presented with pairs of sentences and must predict whether the second sentence is the subsequent sentence in the original document. In about 50% of the cases, the second sentence is indeed the following sentence (labeled as 'IsNext'), while in the other 50%, it is a random sentence from the corpus (labeled as 'NotNext').

For example, BERT might be presented with the pair of sentences "The quick brown fox jumps over the lazy dog" and "They race across the field," and must predict whether the second sentence logically follows the first. The model learns to understand the coherence and flow of information in text passages through this binary classification task.

How "Masked Language Modeling" works

Imagine we have the sentence pair as shown in Figure 10.17 (below)

The cat chased the mouse. It was a fast chase.

Figure 10.17: Input sentence pair used for masked language modeling in BERT

This input sentence pair is then standardized as per required by BERT using the special tokens like [CLS] for class, [MASK] for masking, [SEP] for segment/sentence separation, and [PAD] for padding to make all training samples of equal size. The masked sentence pair is transformed as follows:

[CLS] the [MASK] chased the mouse [SEP] It was a fast [MASK] [SEP] [PAD]
Masked words: (cat, chase)

This masked and standardized sentence pair is then fed into the BERT model and trained using multiple Encoder layers and running multiple iterations or epochs, as shown in Figure 10.18. At the end of a training cycle the BERT model predicts the masked words as "cat" and "chase". The model also tries to predict if this sentence pair has a logical continuation of a previous sentence pair using the flag "IsNext".

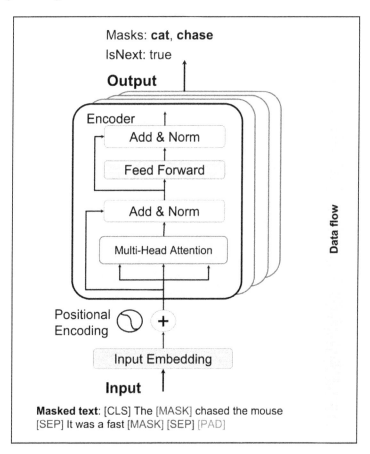

Figure 10.18: Encoder architecture processing a masked sentence for language model training.

In this section we will explore various components and pieces of BERT so that we can understand what goes on in each step of BERT. We will use some predefined training examples to probe the data inside BERT. To make presentation easier, we will flip the model upside down, as shown in Figure 10.19, so the navigation becomes easier. Also, for simplicity we will use only 2 Encoder layers in our model. We will explain the Text Tokenization, Embedding Layer, Multi-Head Attention, the Encoder Layer, and output/Prediction Layer.

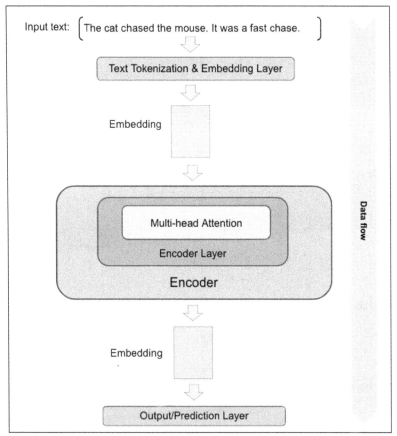

Figure 10.19: BERT Model - Modified/Simplified View

Text Tokenization & Embedding

In BERT, text tokenization and embedding are essential steps that transform raw text into numerical vectors suitable for processing by the model. Figure 10.20 illustrates this process, starting from the input sentence and ending with a structured embedding that captures semantic, positional, and segment information. This diagram shows how words are tokenized, masked, and mapped to embeddings in a way that retains contextual and structural information, which is vital for BERT's deep understanding of language.

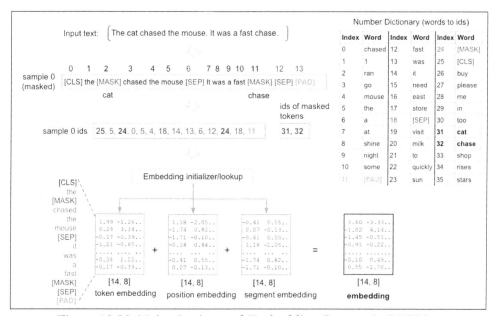

Figure 10.20: Tokenization and Embedding Process in BERT

The figure above provides a detailed view of the tokenization and embedding process in BERT, explaining each component as follows:

1. **Input Text**: The original input sentence is:
   "The cat chased the mouse. It was a fast chase."
   This is the sentence that BERT will analyze. The words **"cat"** and **"chase"** are masked to create a training example that encourages the model to predict masked tokens based on context.

2. **Tokenized Sentence with Masking**: The input text is tokenized and prepared for BERT by inserting special tokens:

   o **[CLS]**: A classification token added at the beginning of the sentence, which BERT uses for overall sentence representation.

   o **[MASK]**: Replaces the masked words ("cat" and "chase") in this example, prompting the model to predict them.

- ○ **[SEP]**: Separates different segments within the input. Here, it marks the boundary between the two sentences.

- ○ **[PAD]**: Padding token added to make the input sequence of a fixed length, which is necessary for batch processing.

3. The final tokenized and masked sentence is:
   "[CLS] the [MASK] chased the mouse [SEP] It was a fast [MASK] [SEP] [PAD]"

4. **Sample 0 (Masked) Token IDs**: Each token is mapped to a unique ID according to BERT's vocabulary. For instance:

   - ○ "the" is mapped to 5 using the Number Dictionary in Figure 10.20

   - ○ "[MASK]" tokens for "cat" and "chase" are assigned IDs 24 and 32, respectively.

5. The sequence of token IDs helps in converting the text into a numerical format compatible with BERT's architecture.

6. **Number Dictionary (Words to IDs)**: The number dictionary provides a reference between words and their assigned IDs. It includes:

   - ○ Common words like "chased," "mouse," "fast," etc.

   - ○ Special tokens such as [MASK], [CLS], [SEP], and [PAD].

7. This dictionary enables BERT to efficiently convert text into token IDs, serving as the foundation for further embedding processes.

8. **Embedding Lookup Process**: The Embedding Lookup process is a fundamental step in preparing input data for a model like BERT. When a sentence is tokenized, each word (or sub-word token) is converted into a unique numerical ID based on a predefined vocabulary. These token IDs are then used to retrieve corresponding vector representations from learned embedding tables. Here's how it works:

   - ○ Token IDs: The input text is tokenized into a list of token IDs.

- o Lookup Tables: These IDs are used to access rows in three separate embedding tables—Token Embedding, Position Embedding, and Segment Embedding.

- o Vector Retrieval: Each token ID fetches:

  - i. A Token Embedding, which contains the learned semantic representation.

  - ii. A Position Embedding, which indicates the token's location in the sequence.

  - iii. A Segment Embedding, which distinguishes between sentences in pairwise inputs.

- o Summation: The three vectors (token, position, and segment) are summed elementwise to produce a single embedding vector for each token.

- o This embedding vector is what gets passed to the BERT encoder, carrying rich information that enables the model to understand not just the meaning of the word, but also its position and context in the input text.

9. Each of these embedding matrices has dimensions $[14, 8]$, where:

  - o **14**: Represents the length of the tokenized input (including special tokens and padding).

  - o **8**: Refers to the embedding dimensions (illustrative size in this example; typically, BERT embeddings are higher-dimensional).

10. **Addition of Embeddings**: The token, position, and segment embeddings are summed elementwise to form the final embeddings for each token. This operation combines:

  - o Semantic (token) information

  - o Positional order (position)

  - o Sentence distinction (segment)

11. This combination allows each token embedding to contain all necessary context for understanding its meaning in relation to other tokens.

12. **Final Embedding Matrix**: The resulting embedding matrix $[14, 8]$ encapsulates the transformed representations of the input sentence. Each row represents a token in the input sentence, enriched with semantic, positional, and segment-specific information. This final embedding matrix is now ready for input into BERT's encoder layers.

This embedding process is crucial as it prepares the text for BERT's deep bidirectional processing, enabling the model to effectively capture nuanced language patterns and context.

Multi-head Attention

The multi-head attention mechanism in BERT enables the model to focus on different parts of the input simultaneously, allowing it to capture various relationships and dependencies between tokens within a sentence. Figure 10.21 illustrates the detailed process of multi-head attention, showing how input embeddings are processed through multiple attention heads to generate a comprehensive context-aware representation for each token.

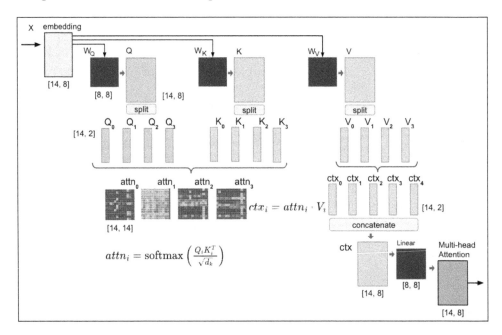

Figure 10.21: Multi-head Attention Mechanism in BERT

The figure breaks down each component in the multi-head attention mechanism as follows:

1. **Input Embedding (X)**: The input to the multi-head attention mechanism is the embedding matrix X, with dimensions $[14, \ 8]$, where 14 represents the sequence length and 8 is the embedding size. This matrix contains the contextual embeddings of each token from the previous layer.

2. **Linear Transformations (Q, K, V)**: The input embeddings are linearly transformed into three distinct matrices: Query (Q), Key (K), and Value (V). These matrices are created using three learned weight matrices:

   o **W_Q**: Transforms the input embedding into the Query matrix (Q) with dimensions [14, 8].

   o **W_K**: Transforms the input embedding into the Key matrix (K) with dimensions [14, 8].

   o **W_V**: Transforms the input embedding into the Value matrix (V) with dimensions [14, 8].

3. **Splitting for Multi-head Attention**: Each matrix (Q, K, V) is then split across multiple heads. In this example, there are four heads, so each matrix is divided into four parts:

   o **Q_0, Q_1, Q_2, Q_3**: Each Query split has dimensions [14, 2], representing part of the total information.

   o **K_0, K_1, K_2, K_3**: Each Key split has dimensions [14, 2].

   o **V_0, V_1, V_2, V_3**: Each Value split has dimensions [14, 2].

4. This division allows each head to focus on different aspects of the sentence, providing diverse attention perspectives.

5. **Attention Calculation (attn)**: For each head, attention scores are computed by performing a dot product between the Query and Key

matrices of the respective head, scaled by the square root of the key dimensions ($\sqrt{d_k}$). The result is a matrix of attention scores (attn) with dimensions [14, 14], where each element indicates the relevance of a token in relation to others in the sequence. The softmax operation normalizes these scores, ensuring that they sum to 1 across each row.

6. **Contextual Representation (ctx)**: Each attention score matrix (attn_i) is multiplied with the corresponding Value matrix (V) to produce a contextual vector (ctx) for each head:

   ○ **ctx_0, ctx_1, ctx_2, ctx_3**: These contextual vectors, each of dimension [14, 2], capture different aspects of the relationship between tokens based on the learned attention weights.

7. **Concatenation of Contextual Vectors**: The contextual representations from all heads are concatenated to form a single matrix (ctx) with dimensions [14, 8], combining the diverse perspectives from each attention head.

8. **Final Linear Transformation**: The concatenated contextual matrix is passed through a final linear layer to project it back into the original embedding space [8, 8]. This produces the final output of the multi-head attention mechanism, which has dimensions [14, 8].

9. **Output (Multi-head Attention)**: The output of the multi-head attention layer, with dimensions [14, 8], is a rich representation of the input tokens, capturing context from multiple viewpoints. This output is then fed into the next layer in the BERT model for further processing.

In summary, the multi-head attention mechanism allows BERT to analyze different relationships within a sentence simultaneously, enabling it to construct a comprehensive, contextually aware representation of each token. This approach is foundational to BERT's success in capturing complex dependencies in natural language.

Transformer Encoder Layer

In BERT, the encoder layer is responsible for building contextualized representations of each token in a sentence. This layer consists of two main sub-layers: multi-head attention and a position-wise feed-forward network (FFN). Each sub-layer is followed by a residual connection and layer normalization, ensuring smooth information flow and stability during training. Figure 10.22 provides a detailed view of the Transformer Encoder Layer, illustrating each step and its components.

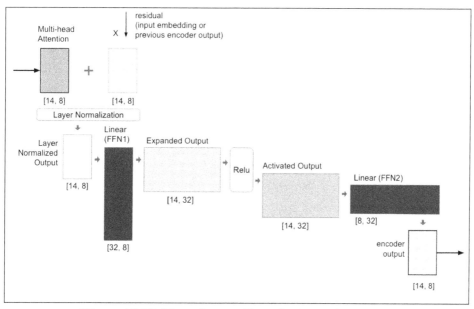

Figure 10.22: Transformer Encoder Layer in BERT

The following explains each part of the encoder layer as depicted in the figure:

1. **Multi-head Attention Output**: The output from the multi-head attention mechanism, with dimensions [14, 8], serves as the input to the encoder layer. This matrix holds the contextually enriched embeddings for each token in the sequence, incorporating information from multiple attention heads.

2. **Residual Connection (Addition with Input Embedding)**: To promote gradient flow and preserve initial information, a residual (or

skip) connection adds the original input embeddings (or previous encoder output) directly to the multi-head attention output. This element-wise addition, resulting in a matrix of $[14, \quad 8]$, helps prevent the vanishing gradient problem and ensures that the model retains initial information across layers.

3. **Layer Normalization**: After the residual connection, the output is passed through a layer normalization step. This process stabilizes the learning by normalizing the outputs, keeping the values within a manageable range and helping the model train more efficiently. The normalized output retains the same dimensions [14, 8].

4. **Feed-Forward Network (FFN)**: The feed-forward network is a two-layer fully connected network with a ReLU activation function in between. This network introduces non-linearity and additional learning capacity to capture more complex features.

   o **Linear (FFN1)**: The first layer in the feed-forward network linearly transforms the normalized output from [14, 8] to [14, 32]. This expansion increases the network's capacity to model complex patterns by projecting the data into a higher-dimensional space.

   o **ReLU Activation**: A ReLU (Rectified Linear Unit) activation function is applied to the expanded output, introducing non-linearity. This transformation results in the **Activated Output** matrix of dimensions [14, 32].

   o **Linear (FFN2)**: The second layer linearly projects the activated output back to [14, 8], returning it to the original embedding dimension. This step compresses the high-dimensional information while retaining learned features, producing an output compatible with the input dimensions.

5. **Encoder Output**: The final output of the encoder layer, with dimensions [14, 8], is a contextually enhanced representation of each token. This output will either serve as input for the next encoder layer (if it's an intermediate layer) or as the final contextual embedding for each token in the sentence.

This structured approach within each encoder layer allows BERT to progressively build a deep, context-rich understanding of each token by stacking multiple encoder layers. The combination of multi-head attention, residual connections, and feed-forward networks enables BERT to model complex dependencies across tokens and capture subtle relationships in natural language.

Output/Prediction Layer

In BERT, the output layer is responsible for producing predictions based on the context-rich embeddings generated by the encoder layers. For tasks like masked language modeling (MLM), this layer identifies the masked words in the input by predicting tokens that fit within the context provided by the rest of the sentence. Figure 10.23 illustrates the steps involved in making predictions for masked tokens, showing how the output from the last encoder layer is processed through fully connected layers to generate the final token predictions.

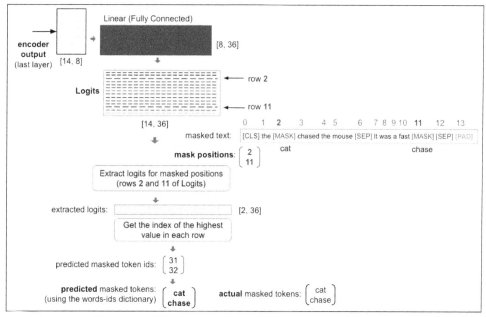

Figure 10.23: Output/Prediction Layer in BERT

The following is a detailed breakdown of each component in the prediction layer as shown in the figure:

1. **Encoder Output (Last Layer)**: The final output of the encoder layer, with dimensions [14, 8], is passed to the output layer. This matrix contains the contextually enhanced embeddings for each token, incorporating information from all preceding layers. Each row in this matrix corresponds to a token in the input sequence.

2. **Linear (Fully Connected Layer)**: The encoder output is processed through a linear (fully connected) layer to map the [14, 8] matrix to [14, 36], where 36 represents the vocabulary size in this illustrative example. Each row in this output now represents the logits (unnormalized probabilities) for predicting each token in the vocabulary.

3. **Logits**: The resulting matrix of logits, [14, 36], contains prediction scores for each token position in the input sequence across all vocabulary tokens. Each row corresponds to a token position in the sequence, while each column represents a specific token in the vocabulary. Higher values indicate a higher likelihood of that token being the correct prediction for the given position.

4. **Masked Positions**: The masked tokens in the input are identified by their positions, in this example at positions 2 and 11, which correspond to the words "cat" and "chase." These positions are marked for extraction, as BERT is tasked with predicting the original tokens in these positions.

5. **Extracting Logits for Masked Positions**: Logits for only the masked positions (rows 2 and 11) are extracted, resulting in a matrix of size [2, 36]. This matrix contains the logits for each masked position across all tokens in the vocabulary.

6. **Prediction by Selecting Highest Logit Index**: For each masked position, the index of the highest value (logit) is selected, as it represents the token with the highest probability of being correct. In this example:

   o For row 2, the highest logit index corresponds to the ID for "cat" (31).

   o For row 11, the highest logit index corresponds to the ID for "chase" (32).

7. **Predicted Masked Token IDs**: The indices of the highest logits yield the predicted token IDs for the masked words. Here, the predicted token IDs are 31 and 32.

8. **Predicted Masked Tokens**: Using the vocabulary dictionary, the predicted token IDs are mapped back to their respective words, resulting in the predictions "cat" and "chase" for the masked positions. This process completes the masked language modeling objective by reconstructing the masked words based on contextual clues provided by the rest of the sentence.

9. **Comparison with Actual Masked Tokens**: Finally, the predicted tokens are compared to the actual masked tokens. In this example, the predicted tokens "cat" and "chase" match the actual masked words, indicating that BERT has accurately filled in the blanks.

This output layer process is crucial for tasks like masked language modeling, enabling BERT to predict missing words based on the bidirectional context in a sentence. By training on such tasks, BERT builds a robust understanding of language that can be fine-tuned for various NLP applications.

BERT represents a monumental advancement in NLP by pioneering bidirectional understanding through the transformer architecture. With its deep, multi-layered approach, BERT captures complex linguistic features, achieving state-of-the-art performance in tasks like sentiment analysis, question answering, and language inference.

Summary

This chapter offers a comprehensive journey through the world of Natural Language Processing (NLP), a key field in artificial intelligence that enables machines to interpret, understand, and generate human language. It begins by outlining real-world applications of NLP—such as machine translation, sentiment analysis, speech recognition, spam detection, and question answering—and explains how NLP bridges the gap between human communication and digital systems. Foundational concepts like syntax, semantics, grammar, and punctuation are introduced to help readers understand how language is structured and interpreted at both the word and sentence levels.

The chapter then walks through practical implementations of NLP using pre-trained models, including a spam detection model and a question-answering system, showcasing how these models tokenize inputs, apply learned embeddings, and classify text based on context and content. Following this, the concept of language modeling is introduced, explaining how models predict sequences of words and capture both syntactic structure and semantic meaning.

A significant portion of the chapter is dedicated to Transformer models and their revolutionary role in NLP. Concepts like word embedding, position embedding, and segment embedding are explored, emphasizing how these contribute to the model's understanding of word meaning, order, and sentence segmentation. The attention mechanism is broken down, first through scalar and then vector-based examples, culminating in the detailed explanation of Scaled Dot Product Attention and how it uses dot products and softmax functions to compute relevance between tokens.

The chapter culminates with a deep dive into BERT (Bidirectional Encoder Representations from Transformers), highlighting its bidirectional nature, masked language modeling (MLM), and next sentence prediction (NSP) strategies. Diagrams and worked examples help illustrate the flow of data through BERT's encoder layers—from tokenization and embedding lookup to multi-head attention, transformer encoder blocks, and the final output layer. The architecture is unpacked in a visually intuitive way, giving readers both a conceptual and technical understanding of how BERT builds powerful language representations.

In essence, this chapter not only demystifies complex NLP architectures but also empowers readers with the foundational knowledge and practical insight needed to understand and work with modern language models like BERT.

Afterword

Throughout this book, we have explored the fundamentals of AI, its real-world applications, and the ethical considerations that come with its power. But knowledge alone is not enough. The true impact of AI lies not just in understanding how it works, but in how we choose to apply it.

AI is a tool—one that can be used to solve some of the world's most pressing challenges, drive progress across industries, and unlock new levels of creativity. But it is also a responsibility. How we build, deploy, and govern AI will shape the future of humanity.

Whether you are a developer, a business leader, an innovator, or simply someone fascinated by the possibilities of AI, the journey doesn't end here. This book is just the beginning. The world of AI is evolving rapidly, and those who continue to learn, experiment, and innovate will be at the forefront of this transformation.

I hope this book has inspired you to explore AI further—to build, to question, and to create. The future of AI is not predetermined; it is in our hands. And it is up to us to shape it for the better.

Acknowledgement

Writing this book has been an incredible journey, one that would not have been possible without the support, encouragement, and contributions of many individuals.

First and foremost, I express my deepest gratitude to my family. Your unwavering belief in me, patience, and encouragement provided the foundation that made this work possible. Your support has been my greatest strength.

To my mentors and educators, who have guided me throughout my journey in AI and beyond—your wisdom and insights have shaped my understanding and fueled my passion for this ever-evolving field. I am deeply grateful for the knowledge and inspiration you have shared.

To my friends and colleagues, who have engaged in countless discussions, offered feedback, and challenged my perspectives—you have helped refine the ideas in this book and made this journey more rewarding.

To the AI and technology community, whose relentless pursuit of innovation continues to inspire and push the boundaries of what is possible—this book is a testament to the incredible advancements we have witnessed and the exciting future that lies ahead.

A special thank you to the readers—whether you are just beginning your AI journey or are already deeply immersed in this field, your curiosity and desire to learn drive the progress of AI itself. This book is for you.

Finally, to everyone who played a role, big or small, in bringing this book to life—thank you. Your contributions, support, and encouragement have made this endeavor not just possible, but meaningful.

With gratitude,

Muneeb Ahmad

www.ingramcontent.com/pod-product-compliance
Lightning Source LLC
LaVergne TN
LVHW081523050326
832903LV00025B/1602